THEATER
OF THE MIND

TALES FROM THE DARKNESS

Ghosts, UFOs, Aliens, Monsters, & Other
Strange Stories of the Supernatural

Dave Schrader

DEDICATION

This book is dedicated to the loving memory of my mother, Terry Schrader, to the living memory of my aunt, Judi Polanowski, and to my biggest supporter when it comes to my writing and storytelling, my dad, Jim Lojewski. Thanks for choosing to be my father and for the constant love and support. This book is for you.

Without the guidance of these three people, I would not be who I am. Thank you from the bottom of my heart.

Special thanks to my editor, Nikki Folsom, and illustration director, Winnie Schrader.

"Show a little faith, there's magic in the night."

— *Bruce Springsteen*

CONTENTS

FOREWORD

Thank you for buying this book in any of its many forms. This book is a labor of love and has been culled from years of exploration and experience.

Many of the stories you are about to read are based on the actual accounts of people just like you. Perhaps as you make your way through these pages, you will even recognize a few stories from my own vast personal history..

I have carefully curated and crafted these tales, cleaned them up, and put them into this readable form so that you can take them along on your journey. May the stories contained within this book be good companions for you and those you share them with, as they have been for me.

Let us begin.

Dave Schrader

1

The Impossible Phone Call

Dallas was buzzing with excitement. The President, OUR President, was in Texas for a visit. There was huge fanfare and a circus-like atmosphere in the city of Dallas, and to say our family were Kennedy supporters would be a gross understatement. We were fervent servants!

My Aunt Evelyn was among the biggest fans of all. Aunt Evy, as we called her, prattled on and on about JFK like he was her own son. I think she may have rivaled even Joe and Rose in the pride department when it came to Jack, as she called him.

It was November of 1963. On this day, our family was knocked out of commission with what I think could only be compared to a version of the Black Plague. We were all down and out, sick, running high fevers, and achy. It was horrible. Aside from that fact, it was just another day in Dallas.

We had congregated in the small breakfast nook in our home to partake in my mother's soup, trying to find resiliency and healing in the ultimate of all comfort foods. The grandfather clock in the hall rang out with a powerful, single BONG to mark the time. It was 12:30 p.m.

A few minutes later, our phone began to ring. Mom stood up, shuffled across the kitchen floor, and grabbed the receiver of our lime green home phone hanging on the wall.

"Benson residence," she chirped.

Immediately, her expression changed.

"I'm sorry, who is this? WHO? Evy, is that you? What are you saying?" She called out, each statement more panicky-sounding than the last.

With great curiosity, we all slowly turned to look at Mom. I don't think anyone took a breath the entire time she held the phone.

"Evy, slow down! Who was shot? Who is dead?" she questioned, then took a long, silent pause.

"When? Oh, my Lord! Wait, what? How is this possible, Evy? How is this possible?" She cried out in desperation and tormented pain.

My father stepped up and approached my mother.

"For God's sake, Margaret, who is that? What is going on?" He barked out.

With that, my mother turned to him. Her eyes rolled straight back into her head. The phone slipped from her hand, striking the floor just moments before she did. Mom collapsed to the ground in a heap, and we all leapt up and ran to her.

Already cradling her, my father was stroking her face, trying to rouse her back to consciousness.

After reaching for the phone to see what was going on and who was there, I was met with an annoying, shrill sound - the same screeching that phones made in that day when left off the hook.

I stood up and replaced the phone on its silver hook, then returned my attention to my parents.

Mom was slowly coming back to us and began shaking quite violently as she cried out.

"Oh, Bob, it was Evy. She said Kennedy had been shot! He's dead, Bob. It was Evy. She said, he's dead!"

She continued to sob.

Trying his best to calm her, Dad held her tightly while gently rocking her in his arms.

"That can't be right, Marge. Evelyn's in a coma, remember? The stroke, honey, she had the stroke," he croaked, sounding as though he was trying to convince himself.

I jumped up, ran across the room, and turned on the bulky old television. We waited with anticipation as it slowly crackled to life. I clicked through the three channels we had at the time, checking each station for a news bulletin. To our surprise, there was no mention of Kennedy, a shooting, or anything of the kind.

"Margie, honey, it was some jackass kid pulling a prank!" Dad assured Mom.

"No, Bob, it was Evy," she sobbed.

Dad called the hospital to check on Aunt Evy. She was there, still very much in a coma and unresponsive.

At that moment, Dad was reminded of his appointment with the doctors the following day. He was required to make a very hard decision about the continued care of our beloved aunt.

The rest of our day, in comparison to the excitement and sense of bewilderment we were left with after the call, was uneventful.

Luckily, Mom eventually calmed down.

The following morning, we went to say goodbye to Aunt Evy as a family. The stroke had been extensive. She was completely unresponsive and lived only with the aid of machines.

I remember the day well and with a heavy heart. It was November 22nd in Dallas, and we were about to say our final farewell to a beloved family member.

We sat in the room, taking turns holding Aunt Evy's hands, sharing fond memories, and shedding a fair number of tears. When suddenly the hospital came to life, there were cries from down the hall. Doctors and nurses filled the rooms. All eyes were on the TV.

At approximately 12:40pm, news began reporting that JFK had been shot and was in transit to the hospital.

We exchanged baffled looks as our mouths dropped open in a state of utter confusion. It had been exactly 24 hours since we received the call from Aunt Evy, my comatose Aunt Evy, that did not have a phone in her room, telling us Kennedy had been shot and was dead.

1 day.....before it happened.

Like the rest of the world, we sat transfixed to the television watching KRLD in Dallas as the story unspool before our very, unbelieving eyes.

We were aghast as the sound of police sirens screamed outside the hospital. They were bringing the president here to Parkland Memorial, where Aunt Evy lay in a comatose state.

The attention of everyone in the room turned to the breaking news from CBS and news anchor Walter Cronkite.

> *"This is Walter Cronkite in our Newsroom," he began. "There has been an attempt as perhaps you now know, on the life of President Kennedy. He was wounded in an automobile, driving from the Dallas Airport into downtown Dallas, along with governor Connally of Texas. They've been taken to Parkland Hospital, where their condition there is as yet, unknown."*
> - Walter Cronkite reporting for CBS TV

Within thirty minutes of Kennedy arriving at Parkland Hospital, Aunt Evy let out a gurgling, sobbing noise as a single tear rolled down her cheek as we watched her slip away.

That was when our attention turned back to the television set and Walter Cronkite.

> *"From Dallas Texas, the flash, apparently official. President Kennedy died at 1 p.m. central standard time, 2 p.m. eastern standard time, some thirty-eight minutes ago.".*
> - Walter Cronkite reporting for CBS TV

Walter Cronkite informed the world.

The rest of what was said was nothing but a murmur of background noise as men and women alike began to sob and comfort one another.

That day, in Dallas, we lost a true American. He was someone who stood for all the things that are good and right in the world - love, family, and commitment to our country.

Oh yeah, and we lost our president too.

I will never forget where I was that day...or the day before Kennedy was killed.

"Time is an illusion."

– Albert Einstein

2

Just Let Go

My name is Jared, and this is my story.

I awoke to a terrifying sensation. A strange chill seemed to envelope my entire body. Trying in vain to open my eyes or mouth, I was unable to move or speak.

As bizarre a feeling as this was, my first thought was an assumption.

"This is the sleep paralysis I always hear about."

I took a long, slow breath, hoping to ride out the uneasy feeling as my faculties returned to me.

At this point, I noticed that through my closed eyes, a blue hue was seeping through my eyelids. My room was no longer dark but lit up in a calming, blue haze.

The cold surrounded me, and it was intensifying. Quickly, it became more bone-chilling, and a sudden, horrifying realization struck me.

"Am I dead? Was this why I couldn't open my eyes, call out, or move?"

I felt the coldness wash over me, caressing me like gentle waves. Despite that sensation, panic began to grow inside me.

I was dead. That would explain the cold, too.

As my mind continued to race, I felt emotion rise up in me like I had never experienced. My throat tightened as thoughts charged through my brain. I would never get to say goodbye to my family, feel my daughter's hand against my face, hear her giggles, feel the warm embrace of my wife, or enjoy the caring and inviting hugs from my mother.

This was it, but I was NOT ready to let go.

I began praying in my head, begging to be put back, to be given one more chance. Panicked, I bargained, promised, and swore my allegiance to God to just spare me, at least long enough to say my goodbyes.

Suddenly, I felt a crackling energy around me.

While I was still ice cold, it felt like low levels of electricity were coursing over the frame of my body. Silently, I screamed inside my dying shell.

"They must be using the defibrillator on me, trying to revive me! God, please let them revive me. Bring me back!"

My eyes began to flutter. I could open them, but my sight was filled with the blue light that had previously creeped through my eyelids. A realization hit me. I couldn't feel my body weight. In fact, I was light and floating.

"No, no, no, no! I am leaving my body...I'm going to the light. The light," I thought to myself.

"I don't want to go to the light. I want to stay here! I HAVE TO STAY HERE!" I kept crying out in my altered state of consciousness.

I have heard that when death comes for you, there will be peace. This, for the record, was NOT peace. It was the absolute farthest thing from it. This was abject terror, and I was not prepared or willing to go.

As I turned my eyes to the extreme right or left, I saw past the brilliant bluish-white glow that now engulfed me. I was hovering in my room and floating toward my window.

As I approached the window, I heard a strange voice. My internal dialogue stopped and was replaced by a forceful, foreign voice that was not mine.

Calmly, it instructed me.

"Just....Let....Go."

Dumbfounded, I began to sob. Nodding my head, I refused, begged, and began to pray. In a move that surprised even me, I jerked my head. Suddenly, I could see behind me.

There, on my bed, sprawled across the covers, my physical form was laying there. Lifeless.

Beside my body, my wife slept peacefully, unaware that I was slipping away. I was dying...or so I thought.

My head lifted, and I squinted towards the light. That was when, through the bright, blue haze, I saw a being beckoning me to let go. It floated just outside my window.

Suddenly, I realized that I was riding atop a blueish beam of light. The figure at my window was imploring me.

"LET...GO!"

I cursed it and begged it to give me one more day.

When my attention shifted briefly, I could hear the whimpering coming from my physical form on the bed.

Jarred back to the moment, I heard it speak to me within my head.

"WHY WON'T YOU LET GO?"

A flood of memories came roaring back through my mind, like a memory tsunami.

Strangely, it felt like a deja vu. I had done this before, seen these beings before. In a dreamlike state, I could remember being very little, then being a teen boy. Other memories from other points in my life flashed before my mind's eye.

I wasn't dying!

The thought only brought me temporary relief because that was when the realization hit me. Without a doubt, I was being abducted.

My mind continued to flood with memories. This had been happening as far back as I could recall. Always the same experience - surrounded by the light, leaving my physical form behind while my spirit-self went elsewhere, only to be reunited later.

Unexpected visions of horror began, flashes of memories - recollections of the beings faces inches from mine, screaming, examining every inch of my ethereal form, shocking and prodding me - only to be followed by the excruciating pain of being put back in my body.

This time felt different, though. I was hovering and struggling against it, even fighting it. They did not like or appreciate my protests at all.

Suddenly, with the force of ejection from a moving plane, I heard the sound and felt the thrust of rushing air, like a gale-force wind hammering me, followed by the unbearable, soul-shattering collision of my spirit form and my physical body crashing violently back together.

My eyes sprung open wide, and my mouth frantically gasped for air to fill my lungs. My chest felt like it would explode.

I sat up, drenched in sweat, and panted like I had run up a flight of stairs. As I turned to roll out of bed, my feet hit the floor with purpose, and I burst forward toward the window.

I saw it.

That son-of-a-bitch was still there, floating outside my window among the inky blackness of the night sky. It was just feet away from me, glaring directly at me with its large, cold, dead eyes. Its hairless brow furrowed in disgust.

Suddenly, there was a flash of brilliant yellow light, followed by a loud sonic sound that exploded around me. Then......
nothing.

It was gone.

I stood there, panting. My chest was heaving, trying to fill with life-giving air as I feebly attempted to regain composure and control over my racing mind.

At this point, my wife sat up in our bed and stared at me.

"Another nightmare?" she inquired.

I asked her if I had them often, and she told me a few times a month.

That was the moment I realized this wasn't a dream or my wild imagination. It was a nightmare of hellish proportions. I was forced to admit the truth to myself.

I was...I am...an abductee.

"Two possibilities exist:
Either we are alone in the
Universe, or we are not.
Both are equally
terrifying."

- Arthur C. Clarke

3

Honeymoon of Horror

My wife and I just celebrated our 8th wedding anniversary. Considering what we faced on our first day as man and wife, we are just grateful that we are still alive to tell the tale of this bloodcurdling memory.

Our vow exchange ceremony was unique in that we had a destination wedding. While this was probably annoying for the attendees, my bride's dream was to be to be married on a sun-drenched beach in February on the anniversary of our official coupling, Valentines Day. Being the ever-loving and mindful groom, I set out to make those dreams come true.

After a great deal of planning and organizing, it was a beautiful ceremony, exactly as she envisioned, with around 30 guests surrounding us. Our day was filled with love and a lot of laughter with good friends and family.

We wrapped up the evening and returned to our hotel, conveniently located on the beach. The location was a gorgeous all-inclusive resort, the name of which I will withhold since I do not want to sully their excellent accommodations and customer service with what happened to us that night...further down the beach...away from the safety of our community and the secure boundaries of the resort.

After a nice meal, a few drinks, and some family and friend time, the sun began to set. My lovely new bride looked deeply into my eye and made a romantic request.

"Let's take a nice stroll down the beach at sunset.....alone," she said with an alluring look in her eyes.

As her new husband, I was more than happy to oblige. Nothing could be better than absorbing the beauty of our surroundings while I happily walked hand in hand with the love of my life. Who could ask for a more perfect ending to an already perfect day?

We strolled down the beach, hands knitted together in a loving embrace, occasionally stopping to stare at the colorful reds, oranges, and purples of the sky as night made its way in and daylight bid us a fond farewell.

The gentle sounds of waves and the calls of the seagulls surrounded us as we made our way down the beach. Every now and then, we paused for a kiss before continuing on our romantic walk. Meanwhile, the music from our resort's beach party became more and more faint.

We hadn't walked down the beach for very long, maybe 10 to 15 minutes. Unbeknownst to us, we were apparently heading away from safety and normalcy. Lost in our love and chatting about our future, our attention was drawn a bit further down the beach in front of us to a girl - a girl in a white nightgown. She stood all alone as she beckoned us with a pitiful cry for help. Her hand was outstretched, waving for us to approach and offer her assistance.

My wife and I are caring people, and this girl seemed in distress. With that, we did what any normal, empathetic person would do. We began to pick up our pace and head down the beach. As we approached, she began to back up, waving us on calling to us.

"Help. Please help," she cried out weakly.

Nearly out of breath and with our hearts racing, we eventually caught up to the girl. She stood by the same pier that earlier that day had been dotted with tourists and locals fishing, walking, and sight-seeing. Now, it was deathly quiet. Only the sound of the waves beating the shores and the girl calling out could be heard.

"Hurry, please. We need your help!"

As we got closer to the girl, things began to get more peculiar. She turned and began to walk into the tide, under the pier, waving for us to follow.

Thoughts raced through our heads. "Are we about to see a dead body? Are they refugees that had an accident?"

As she got waist deep in the water, my wife and I stood at the shoreline. Suddenly, a warning sense kicked in. Something was off... really off... about this. That's when the girl spoke with a louder, more commanding voice.

"Come here! Help us! We need your help."

I squeezed my wife's hand a bit tighter. My nerves took over as I began to speak in a strained, slightly cracked voice.

"What is it? What do you need?" I called out to the girl.

She stood there waist-deep in the water and motioned for us to follow. It felt like we were entrenched in a living nightmare.

"Wait here. I'll go," I told my wife. She gripped my hand tighter and shook her head disapprovingly.

"COME HERE. WE NEED YOU!" The girl insisted.

Slowly, we began to back away from the aggressive girl we had come to help. Our sense of empathy was quickly replaced with a sense of dread like neither of us had ever experienced.

"Wait here. We will go back to the resort and get help," I yelled to the girl over the sounds of the waves.

"NO! COME HERE!" she demanded.

We began to back up slowly, our sweaty palms locked together in a grip of fear.

Suddenly, she began trudging her way back out of the water and directly towards us. Her head was now tipped down as she glared at us from under her furrowed brow. Spread across her face was an irritated, almost menacing look.

As the girl cleared the water's edge, she moved toward us swiftly, almost ungodly fast. When she got within six feet of us, our senses entered hyperdrive. Her gaze burrowed through us from under her scowling brow.

"COME HERE... NOW!" She said it in a terrifyingly calm, yet forceful tone.

As she lifted her head, we could fully see the pale white skin of her face and the thin blue lines of veins mapping her steadily angry face. Then we saw her eyes...deep, dark, solid black eyes. Dark, dead eyes are now staring right through us.

We paused for a moment and realized we were holding our breaths. Slowly, we looked at each other with the same idea, then took off back down the beach toward the promise of the safety of the resort and its well-lit surrounding areas.

As we moved quickly back up the beach, I looked down and noticed that the only footprints visible in the sand were those of my wife and me. That's when we stopped for a moment to take stock of our situation. I whirled back around to see how far we were praying that this demon child was not following us.

There she stood - in the darkening night where we left her - at the water's edge, screaming with a tormented rage into the night sky.

I turned back around, put my head down, and continued my running, half dragging my poor, scared wife. We ran until the sound of music and laughter filled the air and tiki torches burned brightly, lighting our way home like a gloriously lit, yellow brick road to Oz.

When we got back to the safety of our resort, we approached one of the servers on the beach and told her about what happened. Still unsure of what really happened, we recommended that security be called to check on the girl, concerned that she may need help or that more people may be in danger.

The server grabbed the night manager. We pointed down the beach, toward the speck of a pier that was barely visible from this vantage point, and filled him in on our experience.

When we finished, he shook his head and strongly advised that we never...ever...stray from the resort's property again, especially at night. He assured us he would see what he could do about the girl, but only after insisting we not leave the property again.

He did not have to tell us twice. There was no way in hell we would go anywhere near that area or leave the resort again, day or night.

The next day, we inquired about what they found and were told no security was sent, and we were again warned not to leave the property at night as the resort could not be responsible for our safety or for the safety of their own staff ,for that matter, if they wandered off the property.

A few years later, we started hearing about the Black-Eyed Children phenomenon. That's when we finally realized what we encountered that night. Now, when we reminisce, we hold each other a little closer as we discuss that evening. Thank God that we trusted our instincts and didn't follow that girl into the water.

"Instinct is a marvelous thing. It can neither be explained nor ignored."

\- Agatha Christie

4

My Friend Seth

Up until a few weeks ago, I thought I was going crazy after having an experience when I was a kid. For 30 years, I have been so stressed by this, filled with concern and worry that I was completely mental. After hearing a similar story recently, I felt compelled to share my tale.

When I was in grade school, I had a friend that we will call Seth. He was a good friend, but very peculiar. The best way to describe him would be that he always seemed to be a bit...off.

His parents were very protective, and because of that, it was hard to get close to him in any real way. They seemed cold, aloof, and unwilling to let their son have or live what I thought was a normal childhood. He was not allowed to play sports, go to parties, or never allowed to have sleepovers.

But that all changed one night.

Seth and I hung around with each other, mostly at school, because, as I pointed out, he wasn't allowed to do much else.

His 13th birthday was approaching, and we talked about some fun ways to celebrate together. He seemed hesitant to get his hopes up, but you could see in his eyes how much he wanted to let loose and have a fun birthday.

Unfortunately, Seth was certain that his parents wouldn't allow him to do so, at least not in any conventional way.

I asked if he was part of one of those weird religious sects where they didn't celebrate birthdays and holidays. He would just shrug and respond defeatedly.

"I guess so."

Seeing the hurt in his eyes and feeling the pain drip off his tongue when he answered, I left it at that without pushing for more information.

To our surprise, his parents invited me over for dinner and to watch television. I decided to go to help my friend have as much fun on his birthday as possible.

It was November of 1988. Shortly after I arrived, the snow began to fall and fall hard. We had dinner, spent some time in his room hanging out, and decided to watch some television.

By this time, the snow had built up pretty well and was turning out to be a full-on blizzard. You could barely see three feet outside the window. This was a classic white-out.

Seth begged his parents to let me spend the night.

At first, they declined and assured me they would get me home safely when the snow let up. Well, that night, the snow had other plans.

The storm kept rolling, showing no sign of relenting. I heard his parents debating the idea of allowing me to sleep over. They kept going to the picture window, looking up at the skies, then shaking their heads.

Finally, I overheard them say that travel would have been dangerous. With that, they decided that it would be fine if I stayed the night, but just one night, and I called my parents.

Seth's parents kept looking to the sky. Their faces almost looked tortured.

Were they really THAT concerned about the snow? Maybe it was the sleepover that bothered them. Or was it something else?

Seth's dad draped an arm over his wife's shoulder and spoke.

"It's just too bad out there. They will never get through. This will all be fine. Everything will be fine."

He sounded unsure, not seeming to believe what he said, but still trying to reassure his wife.

Nothing very eventful happened for the rest of the night. Well, for the rest of the night until well after midnight, that is.

After I borrowed a pair of pajamas from Seth and taught him the fine art of making a blanket fort in his room, we settled in for the night.

The fort was the perfect spot for a few cookies, juice, and some laughs. It wasn't long before we were off to sleep. To be honest, I do not even remember falling asleep. I remember the cookies and juice, then nothing.

At some point during the night, I woke to an intense, bright light illuminating Seth's room. The light streamed in from the windows, and it poured through the cracks in our makeshift fort.

I looked around and realized my friend was nowhere to be found. In that moment, I assumed he must have gone to the bathroom. As I lay there squinting, attempting to shield my eyes from the glare, I remember thinking, "Come on, what was with this light?"

Suddenly, I noticed that my hearing was off. Everything sounded slow, like the ticking of the clock in the hall and my breath. Even when I tried to speak, it came out distorted and weird as I called out to Seth.

"Seeethhhhhh, where are you, maaaaaan?"

The words poured forth from my mouth like molasses dripping slowly from a tree.

After a few more attempts to call out for Seth and his parents, I rolled over and started crawling toward the opening of our blanket fort. Every movement felt like a chore being carried out in painfully slow motion, like I was slogging through quicksand in a futile attempt to move.

My body moved slowly, but my mind raced. Unable to understand what was happening or make sense of any of this, I was terrified. I remember thinking to myself that maybe I was having a nightmare and needed to wake up.

Finally, I made my way to the bedroom door and pulled it open. It moved in slow motion, too. More light streamed through the door, blinding me and surrounding me. I couldn't make sense of this, it had to be a weird dream.

Stepping into the hall, I saw his parents standing silently side by side, facing away from me.

Now, I was in full-blown panic mode.

"What is happening?" I thought to myself.

My eyes grew wide as I watched the strangest scenario unfold. Seth's parents began to.....how do I explain this? ... flicker. They began to flicker like a picture on an old television set, trying to be tuned in.

As the intense light surrounded them, they continued flickering in and out of existence. Slowly, his parents turned to face me. The light stung my eyes as I tried to return their gaze.

"Where is Seth? What is happening?" I cried out in fear.

As his parents continued to flicker in and out, I gradually saw what looked like other figures begin to reveal themselves between the flickering effect. They were small figures with huge heads.

Strangely, they behaved as if they were trying to hide, being cloaked by the image of his parents.

Convinced that I was losing my mind, I closed my eyes tight and began whimpering, wishing I was anywhere but here, right now.

Seconds later, a very loud, thrumming sound began, so loud that it shook the house. Sounds of glasses and plates clanging together filled the space, while pictures on walls and cabinets rattled competitively.

As quickly as the chaos began, it stopped, and I was totally enveloped in silence.

When I opened my eyes, I was in my room..... at home, STILL in the PJs I borrowed from Seth.

Just like the moment of not recalling actually falling asleep, I had no clue how I was suddenly transported to my own room, in my own house, when it seemed just a moment ago I stood in the hallway of Seth's house.

I jumped up and ran downstairs to find my parents. When I did, I asked them what was going on. They, too, were quite shocked to see me come down from my room when they thought I was miles away at Seth's house.

Confused, I tried to explain to them what happened. My folks, bless their hearts, just dismissed it and said I must have been sleepwalking when I came home.

They called over to Seth's house, but the phone just rang with no answer. Not even an answering machine picked up, it just rang.

I knew that there was absolutely no possible way that I had walked all that way....... in my sleep.....in a blizzard.

HOLY SHIT!

Flustered, I went back to my room. All I kept thinking was, what were my parents thinking, and why were they so calm about this."

Suddenly, it hit me all at once. I walked home in the blizzard. If I had actually walked all the way home, my pajamas would have been soaked. Even better, there would be a footpath leading to our house in the heavy, deep snow.

Quickly, I ran to the window and pulled hard on the string to raise my blinds. They clattered as they shot up. I anxiously peered out, looking for evidence of my mysterious snowy trek.

Nothing. No tracks.

I flung around to look at my bed. It was dry. I was dry, and the pajamas I had on were warm.

With all my evidence, I knew I never walked home, but I will be damned as to how to explain how exactly it was that I got home.

As if this wasn't weird enough, Seth never came back to school. His dad got transferred to a job in Ohio, and the family reportedly moved immediately. I never heard back from any of them again.

Years passed, and a few years ago, I decided to use social media and technology to look for Seth online. Unfortunately, I have not been able to find a trace of him. He had an unusual name, and I couldn't find ANYONE with that name anywhere, ever.

Thank you for letting me get this off my chest and unburden my mind on something that has tortured me for years. I feel, for the first time, like a heavy weight has been lifted from me. I'm resigned to believing I had some sort of alien encounter.

Maybe Seth was a hybrid child that went home, where he would fit in better than he did here on Earth. At least, that has always been what I hoped.

After writing this all out, I went outside, looked to the skies, and whispered to him.

"Seth, wherever you are...I hope you are safe."

"Life is not a problem to be solved, but a reality to be experienced."

- Kierkegaard

5

Turned Away

My story begins about 3 years ago, when I reluctantly attended some local metaphysical expos with my wife in hopes of showing her some support for one of her passions. Personally, I was not a believer in any of it, but it meant something to her. It seemed like a small price to pay to attend and make my wife happy.

After a few months, I acquiesced to my wife and allowed her to set up a mediumship reading for me. We approached the practitioner, and after a few brief pleasantries with my wife, she turned to shake my hand. When we touched hands, she popped her head backwards like she had been punched and let go of my hand.

Immediately, she informed us that she would not be able to do the reading because she suddenly felt very ill. Thinking nothing of it, we said our goodbyes and moved on.

We tried again with another medium a few weeks later at a local Mind, Body, Spirit expo near our home. This time, the medium elected not to do a reading, clumsily insisting she was very booked and couldn't accommodate our request.

I found it strange as I looked down on her table and saw the sign-up sheet for readings. There were availabilities all throughout the schedule. This seemed very odd to me, as she obviously had plenty of time slots still available to accommodate us, but, I thought to myself.

"Whatever. Another day, another $50 saved."

It wasn't until the third time that we attempted to get a reading that I finally became incensed at the attitude of this supposed "Woman of the Light," as she referred to herself. She seemed disgusted by my request, and her face displayed a look like she was smelling something rotten when considering it.

We walked off.

My wife was utterly dismayed and could not wrap her head around this string of strange rejections. Irritated, I spun on my heel and headed back to ask why the "Woman of the Light" was so dismissive and quick to push us away. My wife followed closely behind, begging me in a whisper not to confront the woman.

"Phillip Gellner, don't you dare!" she hissed.

"Hey, Esmeralda," I called out. "What's with the brush off? Why so rude, and why the pinched-up face like you were smelling something foul?" I queried.

She bristled at my short and curt questioning. Personally, I think she became even more offended by me calling her Esmeralda because she informed me that her name was Chastity.

"Of course it was," I thought to myself.

Chastity stated that if I really wanted to know the answers to my questions, she would tell me.

After I insisted on some kind of logical explanation, she looked me dead in the eyes and spoke.

"You have a very dark attachment, and I am not willing to make a connection with it or you!" she hissed.

This response caught me off guard.

"What the hell do you mean I have a dark attachment?"

Man, you could have heard a pin drop. It seemed everyone within 100 feet of us stopped what they were doing, and all attention turned to us.

She shot me a nasty glance for embarrassing her.

It pissed me off even more as she then attempted to shush me.

"Why was SHE embarrassed? I was the one shoved aside for some "load of crap" explanation," I thought.

Without hesitation, she looked at me knowingly.

"Let me guess. Short-tempered, always exhausted, no patience, and constant headaches?"

My wife and I were caught by her frankness, and we nodded in unison.

She then turned her gaze to my wife.

"And he wakes up a lot from nightmares?"

Again, we nodded simultaneously.

"You have an attachment, and it goes way back. It's big, dark, and deeply rooted."

Satisfied that she had given a proper explanation, she waved her hand to dismiss us, then turned her back and sent us on our way.

Dumbfounded, I tried to shake it off by delivering a mini tirade to my wife about the fakery of this whole thing. I told her in no uncertain terms that I would not be attending these "waste of time" events with her again.

To my surprise, she agreed that would be a good idea. With that, our conversation was over.

A few weeks later, we suffered a power outage at home due, in part, to heavy rains and storms moving through our area. We were living by tealight candles. I grabbed one and made my way to the bathroom.

After setting the candle on the counter, I was free to go about my business. Once complete, I approached the sink to wash my hands, giving them a good once-over with soap and water. Readying myself to leave, I turned my attention to the mirror, where I was shocked and horrified to see a massive, dark figure looming behind and above me.

It was wispy and smoke-like, but it was a fully formed humanoid figure. I stood there waiting for my eyes to adjust to the light change and trying in vain to calm my nerves at the obvious low-light hallucination that I was witnessing.

Suddenly, it shot me a menacing toothy grin, leaned over my shoulder, and looked me in the eyes through the mirror's reflection. I could swear that I felt its icy, heavy hands on my shoulders.

My breath was labored as panic began to rise in me.

I tried to collect my thoughts, which seemed nearly impossible with the terror level in me steadily climbing. This was no dream; this was no hallucination. I could feel its hot breath on my neck and its claw-like hands on my shoulders. When I opened my mouth to scream, it began to smile wider - a twisted, crooked smile.

Terrifyingly, it seemed to enjoy my fear.

My blood ran cold as I heard a low, rumbly laugh in my ear.

Then it all went black.

Unconscious, I hit the floor of my bathroom hard.

I have never been able to bring myself to tell my wife what happened. To this day, I refuse to look into mirrors in low light or candlelight.

Every night as I lay in bed, the instant the lights go out, I squeeze my eyes closed and will not open them till the morning light fills my room.

All that runs through my mind is, "What is this, and why is it with me?"

Unfortunately, I am too terrified to tell anyone about this or ask for help because the three times I attempted to speak to someone with abilities, I was quickly shunned.

What does this mean not only for the rest of my life but also for my afterlife?

I am left wondering, in what version of heaven will I ever be allowed to enter, knowing that attached to me there is a very dark passenger.

And what about my wife? Will she ever be truly safe?

"Everyone is a moon and has a dark side which he never shows to anybody."

— Mark Twain

6

Beware The Bloody Bones Man

As a kid who grew up in the 80s, my childhood was relatively normal. I loved the music, sports, girls, and the movies. It should be noted here that I also shared a bedroom and a bunk bed with my little brother, Richard. I slept on the top bunk, and my brother slept on the bottom.

We had a close relationship. I love my brother, and he loves me. We stood by and stood up for each other our whole lives, and still do.

One fall night in about 1986, we had a great day of hanging out and playing after school, where we were involved in a pick-up game of touch football that had thoroughly exhausted us.

We returned home and sat down to dinner with our parents - you know, the way families used to do - talked about the day's events, the game, and school.

After dinner, we settled in for a night of television and general chit-chat.

Eventually, bedtime rolled around. This was a rare night for us where we were not trying to negotiate for 10 more minutes or one more show. We were so wiped out, and sleep sounded so good.

We brushed our teeth, threw on our PJs, and climbed into bed for the night. My brother, being a few years younger, still preferred having a nightlight burn in our room. Personally, I was not a fan because I liked it dark - well as dark as it could be with the streetlight positioned not far outside our second-story bedroom window. It got dark enough, but just enough light came through to cast a comforting gray contrast to our room.

On this specific night, I begged my brother to turn off the nightlight, so I could fall asleep faster. He reluctantly agreed and switched it off. We whispered for a bit and giggled, trying to keep it quiet enough not to alert the parents we were up, but loud enough that we could hear each other.

Finally, sleep overtook us.

A few hours into our slumber, I was roused awake as I felt the bed begin to rock a bit. I was facing the wall and knew what to expect next. My little brother had a habit of climbing up and sleeping next to me if he got scared or wasn't feeling well.

I felt the familiar motion of the bed as he climbed the ladder to join me, then felt the blankets lift as he slid in next to me. That is when I heard something that stopped my heart for an instant…My little brother began to speak.

"Jace, are you there? I heard you climb up there. Are you okay?"

The voice of my little brother was coming from underneath me.

I couldn't breathe. I couldn't talk. I just laid there, trying like hell to figure out what was going on.

Obviously, I had to have misheard him. The voice had to be behind me, but the way I was lying made it sound like it came from beneath me.

Then, I thought about his question.

"Am I there?? He heard *me* climb up??"

"Jace...Jace...why aren't you answering me?" He softly whispered.

I gathered up my courage and whispered back.

"I am fine. Go back to sleep," then I waited for his reply trying to pinpoint where the voice was coming from.

"Jace, why did you leave the closet door open? You know, I hate that," he grunted.

Again, I told him to be quiet and go back to sleep.

Slowly, I rolled over to face what I hoped was my brother.

There, lying next to me in my bed, was a man or a creature - whatever the hell it was. It looked like his skin had been removed from his face and shoulders, leaving a mass of blood-red muscles visible. Silently, it lay there...staring at me. Its eyes did not blink.

All I could hear from within my room was the gentle breathing of my brother below me and the tick, tick, ticking of the clock on the wall.

Not knowing what to do, I froze, laying there face-to-face with this bloody, horrifying creature. I wondered for a moment if this was a nightmare...it had to be. I tried unsuccessfully to convince myself.

The creature had the basic look of Freddy Kruger, but was different - so much different. His eyes were wide and dead, slightly fogged over. His lips were curled back in a Cheshire cat-like smile.

I felt dizzy and nauseous. Every muscle in my body begged to leap up and run away, but I knew I couldn't get past this thing.

It just continued to lay there, staring and smiling like it knew every thought in my head and was relishing the horror I was feeling.

As I opened my mouth to scream for my parents, the creature's bony hand slid up slowly, and his pointer finger pressed to my lips as he hissed.

"Shhhhhhhhhhh!"

I lay there for what felt like eternity, staring blankly into its cold, uncaring eyes as the damn tick, tick, tick, of the clock continued. I'm not sure if I breathed more than a few times during this terrifying ordeal.

It never spoke or moved again. It just...watched me.

Finally, I could see the early stages of sunlight breaking through our curtains. That was when I decided and somehow summoned up the courage to close my eyes and roll away from the bloody bones man.

I held my breath and awaited my fate.

Nothing.

The next thing I felt was the blankets behind me fall like someone had lifted them and let them cascade back down. I heard the creaking of the floorboards in my room, then the moaning of the closet door as it gently closed.

Moments later, the Batman alarm blasted, and my brother and I were now fully awake.

I never made my brother turn off the night light again and began insisting we leave the closet light on at night with the door firmly shut.

Although I never saw the Bloody Bones man again, I would occasionally see what looked like something shuffling around in the lighted closet, through the gap at the bottom of the door.

Finally, I told my brother about my experience when we were off at college, and he visited for a weekend. We got drunk, and I spilled my guts about that night.

That is when he told me about how the Bloody Bones man would stand in the closet when we left it open at night and stare at him from the gap between the door and the doorframe.

Sometimes, it would run its hand up and down the door as it watched us. A silent, scary sentinel was always watching. That was why my brother always insisted on closing the closet door.

I am in my 40s now, and I still sleep with the closet door shut and a light burning brightly inside. I do not think I could ever sleep any other way again.

"Don't be afraid of being scared. To be afraid is a sign of common sense. Only complete idiots are not afraid of anything."

- Carlos Ruiz Zafón

7

Who Wants To Play With Emily?

With the work I do, I can often be found at paranormal conferences interviewing, investigating, lecturing, or simply chatting with patrons. It was at one of these events that this experience occurred.

Following a presentation on Nightmare Creatures that I had delivered to a fervent audience of supernatural enthusiasts, I returned to my vendor table, a place I could easily be found, and approached for pictures, autographs, and copies of my first book, The Other Side: A Teen's Guide to Ghost Hunting and the Paranormal.

After several meet-and-greets, posing for pictures, and signing books, I excused myself to use the restroom. When I returned, I found a small cardboard box on my table, with writing scrawled across the top.

For Dave Schrader.........

Inside the box, there was a handwritten letter. Under the letter, I revealed a doll. Carefully, I reached in and turned the doll to face me.

What I saw next sent shivers down my back and still raises the hairs on my arms at the mere thought of it.

I thought to myself, "this must be a joke because those eyes...those eyes were staring right through me, unnerving me to no end, to say the least." I lifted the letter to read in hopes of uncovering the story behind this horrific little plaything.

Mr. Schrader,

I have heard you offer to take items with a haunted past. This doll, Emily, has been with us too long already, and I am hoping you have an idea of how to deal with her.

It started off simple enough. I had taken my family to a bustling flea market in the town of Anoka, MN, (which you may or may not already know) is the Halloween capital of the world. We walked along looking through boxes and tables of items on display for sale. I was rummaging through a few boxes of old license plates; I had a pretty large collection dating back to the 1930s and was always on the lookout for new ones to add to my ever-expanding collection.

As expected, every now and again, my kids would

approach me with some items of interest that they hoped I would buy for them. My daughter, Caroline, had been pretty good during the day and asked me if I would mind getting her a doll she had found. At this point, she informed me that the doll's name was Catherine with a "C", not a "K," and she would love to bring her home to join the family.

The doll was around three dollars, so I nodded, agreed that it would be fine, and I would purchase Catherine with a "C" for her. She laid the dolly on the top of the items I had already collected from this vendor to purchase, and then she wandered off to join her mother in exploring the flea market.

The vendor tallied my items, and I handed her thirty dollars. She quickly bagged up our goods and sent me on my way. I returned to my car to put the bags I had accumulated in the trunk and returned to the flea market to find my family. We had a great time, and after a few more hours, we decided it was time to go home and find places for all our newfound treasures.

A bit more than halfway home, my car began to shake and tremble, soon followed by a loud noise and the inevitable sound of fwap, fwap, fwap, of a blown tire. I did all I could to maintain control of the car and realized I blew my left passenger tire, forcing me to limp off to the side of the road to change the tire and assess the damage.

I opened the trunk, and that's when I noticed all the bags had shifted off to the left side, but there, laying on top of the spare tire, was my daughter's doll. I surmised that it must have fallen out of the bag when we were driving. I grabbed it, tucked it back in the bag and removed the spare and my jack.

Wouldn't you know it? My spare was flat as well. I made a quick call. Triple A eventually arrived and got us back on the road. We got home and divvied up our items.

That was when I called out to my daughter to come and retrieve her doll. Imagine my shock when she entered the room and squinched up her face before brashly announcing that the doll I was holding was in fact, NOT Catherine with a "C".

Caroline became very upset and demanded that we return the imposter doll to the flea market and get her doll back. I tried explaining to her that the flea market was closed and wouldn't be back open for a few weeks, but I agreed to take her back to return the doll if she wasn't happy with her new friend by then.

I figured after 2 weeks it would be a non-issue, and she would have accepted this new doll and been happy to keep her. My daughter agreed and snatched the new doll into her somewhat hesitant arms and made her way up the stairs - well, most of the way up the stairs.

That is when I heard the thump, thump, thumping of her little body falling back DOWN the stairs. She hit the landing at the bottom of the stairs hard and let out with a wail that could break even the toughest man's heart.

I ran to Caroline and found her arm bent at an impossible angle. My poor little angel had broken her arm and dislocated her little shoulder.

I lifted her in my arms, and we sped off to the hospital, where they reset and cast her arm and shoulder in a long, painful experience. This had become a very LONG day turning into an even longer night. When we got back home, I carried my little girl to her room and laid her down to sleep. There I found that her new doll was sitting prominently on her bed, eagerly awaiting my daughter's return.

"Look," I told my daughter with a smile, trying to sound as upbeat as I could, considering the circumstances, "it's Katherine with a K, and she will keep you company."

With that, my daughter tossed the doll to the ground and informed me, "That is NOT a Katherine, with a C or a K. Her name is Emily!"

And with that exclamation, my daughter made it clear, she didn't want Emily on the bed, and tossed the doll to the floor.

A few hours later, I was stirred from my sleep by the

loud THUD that rattled the rafters from upstairs and then the house was filled with the pitiful wailing cry of my daughter that followed.

My daughter had rolled off her bed in her sleep landing on her sore shoulder and broken arm. It was heartbreaking to see her gasping and sobbing in inconsolable pain, with huge dollops of tears streaming from her eyes.

As I lifted her back to the bed, I was surprised to see Emily was sitting there, right next to where moments ago Caroline had been lying. I guess she must have had a change of heart after all, or so I thought.

Caroline cried out, "No, Daddy! I don't want Emily in my bed!" and again tossed her to the floor. It was with that action, that things were about to get worse, so much worse.

A week passed, and it was a rough one. As a matter of fact, that might be a slight understatement. It seemed like anything that could go wrong for my daughter did go wrong for her, tripping, bumping her head, a mysterious black eye.

I was starting to worry that the neighbors would think I was abusing my daughter. That's when I began to take notice that every time something bad happened that resulted in my daughter being hurt, that damned doll was always close by.

I shook off my suspicious thoughts internally

declared them ridiculous and tried to go about my life.
That is until the night I saw my little girl standing there,
mostly out of her room, throwing me kisses and telling
me good night before she would go crawl into bed like
every other night.

What I saw next was horrifying on so many levels. I
saw her little hand that was grasping the door frame, her
lithe, little body leaning out, her face bright and sweet
as she smiled at me. All of a sudden, I saw the door
slam, catching Caroline's little fingers between the door
and the door frame. She burst out, howling in pain.

I ran to her and assumed one of my other kids must
have been in there horsing around and accidentally
shutting her little fingers in the door. When I threw open
the door, the room was empty, except for that damned
doll, sitting suspiciously close to the door, and a terrified,
wounded little girl, sobbing uncontrollably.

I know this all sounds crazy, but after my wife and I
tended to my daughter's bruising hand and fingers, I
tucked her back into bed and grabbed the doll roughly
by its arm on my way out of the room.

I lifted it to my face and growled in its face as I stared
deep into its cold, dead glass eyes, "You...Are...Gone!"
I barked, pausing between words to emphasize my
resolve.

"You are nothing but bad luck." I continued as I
brought her to my garage and wrapped her in a blanket that

I kept in the trunk of my car, and slammed the trunk aggressively, feeling as though I had just slayed a dragon. I was now determined to return this jinxed toy and get Catherine with a "C" for my daughter while returning Emily with an "E" for evil back to the flea market, where it belonged, and where it could become someone else's problem.

The following week, the flea market was back up and running. I drove down with my daughter in hopes of finding the doll she actually wanted and to return the devil doll we had gotten by mistake. Thankfully, it had been an uneventful week; no broken bones, no bruises, and no night terrors from Caroline.

This nightmare was finally coming to an end, but to my utter horror, when I opened my trunk, I found Emily, lying there, unwrapped, far from the blanket she had been bundled in, and that's when I saw her eyes.

Something had happened to Emily - something frightening. I tried to convince myself that it must have been the heat and humidity of being stored in my trunk, but her eyes had changed. They were red, not kind of red but a VERY dark, sinister shade of red. Seeing this, I immediately felt sick to my stomach.

I then thought, "Wait, was her brow furrowed a bit more than before, making her look even more menacing? Without much thought, I slammed the trunk, and together, Caroline and I raced back to the flea market before something else could happen.

I approached the vendor with my daughter in tow. I could not get to him fast enough. As we approached, thankfully, sitting atop the display case was Catherine with a "C" and we were met by a very smiley vendor.

He greeted us with a warm grin and, to my total confusion, he said, "I'm glad you came back. You forgot your doll you paid for last time."

I informed him that somehow the dolls had gotten switched, and I handed him Emily. He gave the doll a quick once-over and then told me in no uncertain terms that was NOT his doll, and handed both Emily and Catherine back to us. We were shocked, and I was left wondering how the hell that creepy doll got into our bag?

We returned to the car, and I placed both dolls back in the trunk for the car ride home. My mind felt cloudy, I was so confused, and Caroline kept insisting she did not want Emily and that we should just get rid of her. I tried to maintain a look and sense of comfort for her, but she verbalized exactly what I had been thinking the entire drive home.

When we pulled into the driveway, I opened the trunk to retrieve Catherine and had decided to just throw Emily away. When the trunk latch popped, my heart sank in my chest. There, sitting dead center in the trunk, Emily was next to Catherine, who's pretty little porcelain face had been crushed beyond repair. Caroline was heartbroken as she sobbed and ran into the house.

I didn't know what to say; What could I say? I had a killer, jinxed doll?

That's when I remembered you, Mr. Schrader. So, I wrapped her up, stuck her in the box you now hold, and knew she had to go. She has been in my trunk in a box since that day. I opened it just to slide this note in and make sure the damn thing was still in there, then taped it shut.

That's my story, and YES, I am sticking to it. Goodbye, Good riddance and Good Luck, Mr. Schrader.

Thanks for taking care of this.
J.L.

****

After reading this disconcerting tale, I did as I always do. I took the doll home. When I arrived with a box, I was met with a lot of curiosity from my daughters' wanting to know what I had gotten them.

I explained to them that it was a reportedly haunted doll and that a listener dropped it off to me. My plan was to wrap the doll in bubble wrap and stick her in the far side of our garage along with her other satanic siblings I store out there, among the many other disgruntled paranormal experiencers that had dropped off their possessed possessions with me.

My girls demanded to see it.

After a few minutes, I relented and told them they might be sorry. They laughed and rolled their eyes at me until I drew Emily out of her box and turned her around.

The blood-red eyes effectively freaked them out, as well as my wife, who insisted we just go toss the thing in the trash right now.

I decided instead to wrap her in blessed bubble wrap, box her up, and store her away - far from where she could do harm to anyone. All the while, I laughed inside at how ridiculous this whole thing seemed and how far-fetched these claims were.

At the same time, I learned long ago not to summarily dismiss stories like these but to instead keep these stories, curate them, and store the items in a safe place.

From time to time, I will go out to the garage and visit these strange curiosities, catalog them, and return them to their boxes. That is exactly what I planned to do seven or eight months later as I strode, unknowingly, to my garage with pad, and paper in hand.

When I flipped the light on and approached the back of my garage, I was stunned to see Emily, sitting atop the closed box of dolls, no longer swaddled in the bubble wrap. Even more curiously, the box in which she had been stored was closed. By closed, I mean closed and still sealed with tape.

I wrapped her up again, and placed her back in the box, and placed another box on top.

A week later, the box on top had toppled to the floor, and Emily sat atop the box of dolls.

As far as I know, she has not hurt anyone. Additionally, I cannot say with full knowledge that she is, in fact, possessed or even truly haunted, but after grilling my kids, they assured me they had not touched her, nor would they want to. Taking all this into account, I decided it was time for Emily to go.

Now I ask you, dear reader, "Who wants to play with Emily?"

"From ghoulies and ghosties and long-leggedy beasties and things that go bump in the night, Good Lord deliver us."

– A Scottish Prayer

8

Hand In Hand

During the summer of 1996, I went on a long weekend adventure with my best friend, Barry, and our girlfriends, Katie and Marie. Personally, I was not a fan of long car rides because they often made me sick, so I did my best to try and sleep as much as I could through them. They say the true reward is the journey, not the destination. I, however, strongly disagree.

We had spent an extremely fun weekend at Barry's Uncle's cabin, where, thankfully, we did not encounter any machete-wielding, masked psychopaths hunting us down one by one.

That weekend, we fished, hiked, and spent a lot of quality time cuddling by campfire with our girls as we shared many laughs and exchanged ghost stories. All the while, we were surrounded by the harmonic call of nature and the comforting sounds of a gentle fire crackling and popping.

I listened intently as each of my three fellow travelers shared their strange experiences with the supernatural. Up to this point,

I had not been so lucky as to have my own experiences to share, but I listened in wide wonder.

If I'm being honest, most of the stories seemed "pretty out there" and hard for me to believe, but I was struck by the tale that Barry shared involving his grandmother.

A few years earlier, Barry was asleep in bed at his home and had been awoken by someone patting him vigorously, trying to get his attention. He slowly sat up in bed, rubbing his eyes and stretching out his balled-up fists into a yawn and stretch. When he opened his eyes, he was surprised to see his grandma standing there beside the bed.

Barry rubbed his eyes a bit more, trying to will himself awake.

"Hey Grandma, I wasn't expecting you. What a nice surprise. What are you doing here?"

She smiled at him and began to wave. As she did this, he said she began to dissipate, just like a wispy cloud breaking apart. It began slowly at first from her feet and ran all the way to her head until there was nothing left but a shocked and bewildered grandson in an empty bedroom.

At this point, Barry was now fully awake and ran from his room, down the hall, and into his parents' room to tell them what he had just witnessed.

After listening to the experience, his father dismissed him with a wave and a grunt as he lay back down, but his mom, showing more concern, said she could see Barry's fear and confusion.

The two of them went to the kitchen and decided to call his grandparents to do a quick wellness check on everyone. It was late, and the phone rang and rang, which was expected as they had not caught up with the times. They did not have cell phones, and the only telephone was still mounted on a wall in the kitchen.

After two or three attempts, they decided to call it a night and try them again first thing in the morning.

Two hours later, Barry's household was startled awake by the sound of the hall phone ringing. He heard the gentle padding of his mother's feet making her way down the hall to answer the call. He could only hear one side of the conversation.

"Hello?"

"Oh no, Daddy, no…" then she quietly began to weep.

Barry got out of bed. As you probably guessed, it was his grandfather calling to say grandma had passed silently in her sleep. They had been enjoying a short vacation and were not at home, which is why they had not answered the phone earlier when Barry and his mother had tried calling.

As Barry told the story, I could see the faraway look in his eyes. He was mentally right back in that moment, reliving the experience as he relayed it to us. His voice sometimes quivered in a mix of sadness and puzzlement over what he had seen and witnessed that night.

Even now, all these years later, he is still unsure of what really happened. Had his grandmother revealed herself to him before she took that final step away from this mortal existence, or had it all been a dream?

This ghost story, in particular, really touched me in many ways.

I lay awake late into the night thinking of what Barry had shared and how jarring it must have been for him and his family. Considering it for a moment, I wondered what I would have done in the same situation.

The next day, we set off for home, and I settled comfortably in the front passenger seat for the long drive.

About ninety minutes into the trip, the girls began to nod off in the back seat. I was soon to follow, but not before making sure Barry was going to be good on his own as the rest of us slept. He assured me that he would relish the silence after the long, loud weekend that we had all just shared.

I turned sideways in the bucket seat and slung one arm over the back side of the seat. That's when I felt Marie lace her fingers into mine as I drifted off to join her in dreamland.

Sometime later, I woke up to the sensation of Marie's hand in mine. Her fingers were cold as ice. I gave her hand a gentle but firm squeeze and quietly called back to her.

"You OK, babe?"

There was no answer, so I gave her another squeeze while tugging her arm a bit trying to rouse her.

I called out again.

"Babe?"

Still no answer.

Barry saw the concern on my face and glanced back into the backseat. He assured me that both girls were still fast asleep.

Meanwhile, I couldn't believe how coldly her hand was clutching mine.

Suddenly, a sense of panic overtook me, and I squeezed her hand harder, yanking her arm.

"Marie! Baby, are you OK?" I cried out in an anxiety-filled voice.

To my surprise, she sat up and quickly assured me she was.

While I was looking at her, I was shocked beyond belief. She was rubbing her eyes - with BOTH hands!

Katie, Barry's girlfriend, was beside her in the far driver's side back seat. She was definitely out of my grasp, yet I could still feel my hand entwined with an icy cold, hand.

Immediately, I let go of the phantom limb and let out a yelp. In response, Barry damn-near ran us off the road as he pulled the car into a screeching halt on the shoulder.

After we were safely pulled over, I began to excitedly explain what had happened and why I was so freaked out. That's when I took notice of Barry's face.

It went completely white. His jaw was agape, and he was wide-eyed in shock.

My whole world turned upside down as Barry revealed even more information about the story that he had shared last night at the campfire.

The car we were driving in at that very moment belonged to his grandparents. The backseat where the girls were now sitting is exactly where his grandmother had passed in her sleep while his grandfather, unaware, drove through the night.

My skin crawled as the realization washed over me that I had just been holding hands with a ghost.

As I said earlier, this story really touched me...in many ways.

"The people you love become ghosts inside of you, and like this you keep them alive."

- Rob Montgomery

9

Sleep of the Damned

Dr. Andrew Nichols is the former Director of the American Institute of Parapsychology. He holds a doctorate degree in clinical psychology and is the author, co-author, or editor of more than fifty research papers, popular articles, and books on paranormal topics.

Over his expansive career, Dr. Nichols investigated more than 600 cases of reported haunted houses and poltergeists.

This story was relayed to me directly from his own first-hand experience. I would like to thank him for allowing me to share his encounter in this book.

As a parapsychologist, I am often asked if I have ever been really frightened during an investigation. I have certainly spent many nights in dark cellars, dusty attics, and deserted European castles, but I can honestly say that I have rarely experienced anything that I found particularly scary. I have witnessed apparitions and poltergeist activity on several occasions, and although these experiences were startling and fascinating, I never regarded them as personally threatening.

Most haunting investigations are rather tedious and involve hours and hours of waiting for something...*anything*, to happen. However, some years ago, I suffered a particularly terrifying sleep-related experience following my investigation of a poltergeist disturbance.

The case involved the phenomena typically associated with such events - unexplained movement of objects, percussive sounds emanating from the walls and ceiling of the home, and (somewhat unusual) sightings of amorphous, shadowy apparitions.

The 'epicenter' of the phenomena appeared to be centered around an 11-year-old girl with emotional problems.

The family believed their home was haunted by a 'demon.'

In view of subsequent events, I am forced to admit that the family's simple religious explanation may be closer to the truth than my 'scientific' one.

I have investigated several such cases during my four decades of psychic research and, like most academically-oriented parapsychologists, had always tended to attribute such disturbances to the unconscious projection of paranormal energies from a human agent, described in parapsychological jargon as *recurrent spontaneous psychokinesis* (RSPK). My experience with this case led me to seriously reconsider the 'spirit hypothesis' as a possible explanation for some haunting and poltergeist cases and to re-evaluate certain cases of alleged 'demonic possession' as well.

I had gone to bed along with my wife after a day of investigation at the home of the poltergeist-infested family. Sometime in the early morning, I 'awakened' to find myself in the midst of an out-of-body experience. I found myself floating face down, about four feet above my physical body. I could clearly see the details of my sleeping body below, lying on my back, and my wife sleeping on her side, facing away from me. Previously, I had a couple of OBEs (out-of-body experiences), but none as vivid as this one.

Delighted, I wanted to maintain this wonderful sensation as long as possible. As I hovered there in mid-air, I contemplated an attempt at 'astral travel' to discover if I could project my etheric body to some distant location. It was that moment that the experience turned into a terrifying struggle for my sanity and – corny as it sounds – my *soul*.

Unexpectedly, the eyes of my sleeping body below me opened. The eyes (*my* eyes!) were completely black. No pupils, no iris, just a jet-black sclera, pools of blackness staring back up at me.

I knew instantly that those eyes could *see* me, although I was also certain that my floating astral body would have been invisible to anyone else standing nearby. In addition, I had an absolute certainty that *something* had taken possession of my body and that the thing – whatever it was – could see me perfectly well.

That was when my body below began *grinning at me - a sly, sinister grin*. It seemed to be enjoying my terror, and I was instantly aware of two things:

First, I knew I had to get back into my body very quickly, or I would be forever displaced by this entity, which, I had absolutely no doubt, was *evil*.

Second, somehow (telepathy perhaps?) I knew that this thing intended to harm my wife.

I began to struggle to re-enter my body, and the feeling was like pushing against an invisible barrier, like the feeling one gets when trying to force two magnets of opposing polarity together. This struggle to reincorporate myself was the last thing I remembered until I suddenly found myself back in my physical body. Except I was no longer lying supine in bed but was crouching over my wife with my hands around her throat as she fought to break my grip, screaming at me to "wake up!"

After we both regained some degree of composure, I explained to her what I had experienced, and that was when she described her version of the story.

She was awakened by the sounds of me groaning and muttering what sounded like a foreign language, which she did not recognize. She assumed I was having a nightmare. When she tried to awaken me, I attacked her, my eyes wide open and apparently growling at her like a rabid dog.

She said that the voice that emanated from my body was deep and gravelly, totally unlike my own, and the expression on my face she described as "leering and hateful." My attack only lasted for a few seconds before I came to myself again.

Now, my wife is not a shrinking violet. She has for many years suffered from a husband who spends his time 'chasing spooks', but this was just *too much!* She informed me sternly that if my episode had lasted for a few more moments, she would have treated me to a broken nose.

To this day, I am amazed that I didn't spend the rest of my married life sleeping on the couch; however, my long-suffering spouse seemed to take the experience in stride. Although I assure you, she slept with one eye open for some time afterwards. Thank God there have been no recurrences of this condition of 'possession.'

So, was I actually 'possessed' by some dark spirit?

I am a long way from being convinced. Although I confess, I can't dismiss the possibility either.

I can't state with scientific certainty that this experience was anything other than a particularly vivid and horrific nightmare. I have no witnesses other than my wife, and there is no evidence that this was anything other than subjective.

Certainly, my psychologist colleagues would dismiss the incident as a dream – a variation of the 'night-terror' syndrome, possibly induced by anxiety associated with my involvement with the poltergeist case. Psychoanalysts would probably also speculate that repressed hostility toward my wife may have been at the root of the experience.

I cannot offer any evidence to contradict these explanations, but the experience was so terrifying, so *real*, that I can't help wondering if the Spiritualists' interpretation of possession is closer to the truth.

"There are more things in heaven and earth, Horatio, Than are dreamt of in your philosophy."

– *William Shakespeare from Hamlet*

10

High Strangeness

It started off like you would expect, little things at first. My keys would go missing and end up in my mailbox, the television would turn on and off by itself, and then came the subtle sounds of scratching inside the walls. Of course, I would chalk it up to being distracted and setting things where they don't belong absentmindedly. Perhaps the television thing was just a nearby neighbor with the same brand using his remote and affecting my set. That sound of scratching in the walls, those were surely mice or squirrels that had found their way inside. Right?

I had never been a believer in the paranormal. To me, that stuff was fun to watch at the theater and on television, but I never gave it a second thought or any consideration toward the phenomenon being real.

At the time, I lived with my wife and my then fifteen-year-old daughter, Kia. I never thought to ask them if they were noticing the strange things going on at the house. Maybe I didn't ask because I was afraid of the answer and what that might mean, making things all too real. I mean, we had lived there for seventeen years and NEVER had any kind of problem at all during that time. Unfortunately, that all changed, and things are different now.

I would come down in the morning to fix some coffee and find every cabinet wide open with napkins thrown all over the floor. Our tabletop, which was usually adorned with a lace runner down the middle, a bowl filled with fake fruit, and two sterling candle sticks, one at each end, would all be removed from the table and strewn about the room in a haphazard fashion.

Finally, I decided to address my wife and daughter about the level of high strangeness taking place at our home. Both made the same claim that they had "no idea" what was going on and that they did not have a hand in it.

That's when I started to get this sick feeling in the pit of my stomach. Was someone sneaking around inside our house while we slept at night? It didn't happen often, but a few times a month, I could count on it. We lived in a sleepy little town where a good portion of the time we never bothered to lock our doors or windows.

Just to be sure, I changed all the locks that day and got an inexpensive security camera set up. To be thorough, I placed them by the front and back doors, the kitchen, and just outside my daughter's room to see if perhaps she was sleepwalking or, even worse, sneaking some boy into her room.

Of course, nothing happened for over a month, until the night I was startled awake by the sounds of the kitchen cabinets banging. I switched on the small monitor that was next to my bed and pulled up the video feed from the kitchen. It crackled to life, and the sound of static let out an electronic hum as the picture came into view.

The doors of the cabinets were slowly banging, repeatedly opening and shutting *ALL* of them with different speeds and force. It looked like twelve sets of unseen hands were working each door on their own, with what seemed like anger and frustration.

Silently, I sat there watching; Only the sound of my shallow, short breaths surrounded me. The cabinet doors slowly came to a stop and softly closed. I was stunned. As I sat there trying to understand what I just witnessed, a force like a shockwave rolled through the kitchen, forcing all the cabinets to burst open simultaneously.

I reeled back in horror from the small video screen, and my bed violently lurched, then settled back on the floor with a loud *THUD*!

Trying to make sense of what just happened, I did my best to convince myself that I must have overreacted more forcefully than I had thought in jerking back from the monitor. That had to be what made the bed appear to move on its own.

Just then I began to feel the bed moving - a slow tremor at first, almost clacking on the floor, then two violent slams. Suddenly, as quickly as it started, it stopped. My wife sat straight up, startled.

"What the hell just happened? Are we having an earthquake?"

YES! I thought to myself.

It *HAS* to be an earthquake making the cabinet doors move. Of course. That must have been the early tremors of the coming quake. It made sense. Well, it did until I heard the blood-curdling screams of my daughter Kia tearing the night open from two rooms away.

Her bed was now thumping and bumping. I raced down the hall and threw open her door. My wife and I stopped short, watching with utter amazement at our poor, helpless daughter flailing about, screaming as her bed bucked and banged like a wild bull.

Terrified, I tentatively approached the bed. The need to protect my daughter was slightly, and I mean slightly, more important at that moment. In truth, I hated myself for feeling that way.

As I got closer, I reached for her. Suddenly, the bed slammed hard to the ground and landed on my left foot. I let out a howl and dropped to the floor, writhing in pain, clutching my foot, and doing my best to hold back the myriad of filthy words my mind was lacing together and crying out in my head.

My wife ran to our daughter, yanking her swiftly off the bed and into her protective arms, where they then slipped to the floor together in a sobbing mess of hysteria. They slowly began inching their way closer to me and my throbbing foot.

We barely had a chance to breathe and collect our thoughts when the sharp sound of scratching began filling the room. It sounded like it was coming from under the floor.

Scratching, scratching, scratching.

It was soft at first, then more furious. Interestingly, it seemed to circle us on the floor, then made its way under the bed. That's when I saw the OUIJA board jutting out from under the corner of my daughter's bed.

"WHAT THE HELL?!?" I cried out in shock.

I felt like I was on a hidden camera show. This had to be a prank. I was experiencing every cheesy horror movie cliché that I had ever seen.

Suddenly, the scratching noises stopped, and the room filled with hushed tones of whispers, like being surrounded by an audience at a play waiting for the show to begin.

Soft, indiscernible words were being uttered like we were being observed by an audience of unseen hordes filling the room. The whispers were coming from all around us and were quickly followed by the unmistakable sound of heavy footfalls coming down the hall directly to the room we were in.

We huddled together, unsure of what was about to happen next. My wife's sobs mixed with my daughter's inconsolable crying, all rounded out by the sound of my heavy, panicked breathing.

We could hear the bounding footsteps change course and dart back down the hall, toward the stairs to the kitchen. The whispers - those horrible whispers - stopped as quickly as they had begun.

We slowly stood, and I pointed to our bedroom. My wife looked at me knowingly as she pressed her pointer finger to her lips and shushed our daughter. Then, together and as quietly as we could, in this creaky, noisy old house, we made our way to the master bedroom. Swiftly, I closed the door, locked the handle, and slid my heavy old dresser up against the door.

I reached down and picked up the monitor to investigate the kitchen to see what was making the sounds we heard coming from downstairs. It looked like a man, my size, stomping in a rage around our downstairs living quarters.

The monitor lights flickered, and I saw him move into the kitchen. His head was facing down, and he seemed dazed as he rubbed his head. With the back of his hand, he rubbed at his eyes. When he lowered his hands and turned from the sideways position in which he had been standing, I could clearly see his face.

It was… MY FACE looking back at me. I murmured in utter astonishment while looking at the surreal sight unfolding before me.

"Oh my God!"

It was as though I was watching a video replay of myself stumbling around the kitchen in the morning, bleary-eyed and seeking coffee.

My wife stood by my side, eyes wide, and she whispered in a fit of confused anger.

"Who is that? What's going on? Why is this happening to us?" she asked, each question more frantic than the one before.

I tried to comfort her by placing my arm around her shoulders and pulling her close, praying she didn't push for those answers, as I obviously had none.

"We need to call 911," I mumbled in a state of shock, all the while wondering, what was I going to tell them?

I watched myself roam around my kitchen on a monitor system. Was I going to tell them ghosts were levitating our beds?

Still unsure, I pushed the numbers on my phone, 9-1-1. and hit send. The phone rang once, then a second time. Suddenly, the dispatcher's voice filled my ear.

"911. What is the nature of your emergency?" she asked.

I reported to her that we had an intruder and something strange was going on in our home. As calmly as I could, I informed her that we were hidden in our room upstairs and begged her to send someone quick. While I tried to hang up the phone, the dispatcher insisted on keeping me on the line while we waited for what seemed like forever.

The stillness of the house was shattered by the sound of a pounding on our front door. The dispatcher then informed me that the police were here, asked if I felt safe, and inquired to see if I could make my way down to open the door for them. Unsure of what may be waiting to spring out at me between here and the front door, I agreed with trepidation.

As quickly as I could, I moved across the hall, down the stairs, and rounded the wall to get through the kitchen to the door.

Suddenly, I slammed hard into someone. I steadied myself and then looked directly into the face of the intruder, who looked as shocked as I was.

Standing inches in front of me, I had come face-to-face with *MYSELF*. The only difference I could see was the scar on his upper lip.

I froze in a state of utter confusion. He calmly smiled at me, then began to speak, in a calming, almost reassuring way.

"Ohhhhhh, yeah!" He said it slowly and deliberately, like he was having a revelation of sorts.

"Wow, I remember this. I remember this happening. Man, this is so weird," he finished.

He pointed to my upper lip. Curious, I ran the back of my hand against it and saw that there was a smear of blood. After I pressed my tongue over my lip, I tasted the unmistakable, bitter, coppery flavor of blood that was spurting from my recently split lip.

Everything began to move so slowly. My vision was filled with little white spots, then everything went black. I passed out.

When I woke, I was strapped to a gurney outside an ambulance, surrounded by my wife and daughter, EMTs, and a police officer taking their statements.

They held nothing back and explained every frightening second. That's when he turned to me and spoke.

"Is this what you experienced, sir?"

A look of confusion and disbelief came across his face, and I nodded in agreement. He closed his notebook and walked away.

A few minutes later, the same cop approached my wife and slipped a piece of paper to her.

The EMTs cleared me after they cleaned up my split, bloody lip and comfortably assessed that I was fine to get up and return to my home after assuring us that no one was found in the house.

I stood and asked my wife what the police officer had handed her. She opened her hand slowly to reveal the slip of paper with a woman's name and number scrawled across it. The police officer told my wife he knew of a woman who dealt with this kind of thing, and we should call her and say he sent us.

The police officer also informed my wife that he secretly removed the OUIJA board he found in my daughter's room and gave a strong warning to her and my daughter against playing with those again. My wife quickly agreed and nodded slowly.

We made the call to the woman the kind police officer had referred us to as soon as we could, and after a short explanation of what had happened, we then invited her to visit our home.

A few days later, this lovely lady named Margery made her way through our house, clearing the rooms, burning sage, and praying with us. She said the danger had passed, but from time to time we might still feel little repercussions from our experiences.

Additionally, she indicated that it was okay to be afraid. In fact, it was natural, but it reminded us we were okay now and in control. Finally, she indicated that she would always be just a phone call away.

When asked about the OUIJA board, she said the spirit board mixed with my daughter's age and the tension in our home recently could have been what instigated this whole thing. Surprisingly, she said that she had seen something like this before but assured us not to worry because we were safe now.

Before leaving, I asked her about seeing myself. She smiled and said, "Time is a funny thing….. but don't be surprised if one day, while making my coffee, I run into a very exasperated version of myself entering the kitchen very quickly."

She then assured me to just take it in stride, as it would pass quickly.

So now, I wait…fully aware that sometime in the future I will encounter this situation from an entirely different perspective.

The next chapter in this little saga, I believe, is going to be very interesting.

"There are a lot of things we don't understand, and many of them are incredibly strange and mysterious."

– Art Bell

11
To Hell and Back

After a life of attending parochial schools, I had a kind of falling out with religion, church, and my faith. It no longer seemed to suit me. I found it silly - nothing more than old superstitions cobbled together as a money-making scheme for churches to get richer and prey upon the lost and impressionable.

I had never considered myself a bad person, certainly no worse than anyone else I knew. Like many others, I am often selfish and not nearly as neighborly or caring as I could be. But who among us couldn't say the same?

When I was twenty-seven, I moved into my neighborhood and never once exchanged words or pleasantries with my neighbors. There was no real contact at all, aside from the occasional nod of the head in passing. All that and everything I knew changed one summer day, a few months after I turned forty-five years old.

I was out mowing my lawn when I felt my stomach start to sour, followed by a strange sensation in my chest. Immediately,

I regretted the gas station burritos that I had scarfed down during lunch.

The heat was getting to me, and I turned off the lawn mower to take a sip of water. That's when it hit me like a thunderous punch from a heavyweight boxer, square in my chest.

My mouth dropped open into a silent scream as I gurgled in pain. My vision began to flutter in and out of focus.

I could hear the distinct sounds of my neighborhood - kids playing, dogs barking, people mowing their lawns. Then…. it all went silent. The only thing I could hear was the offbeat rhythm of my own heartbeat pulsing in my ears.

Throbbing…. throbbing…..throbbing…

Suddenly, the sunlight before my eyes went dark, and I collapsed.

I remember the sensation of feeling like I was laying on my parents' waterbed when I was a child, then slowly light started to flicker into view once more and I began to hear the voices.

"Oh, he's here. Finally, he's here," one voice called out excitedly.

The voice was loud yet hollow, almost like calling to me through a tunnel or long hallway.

Within seconds, I could see a bright light. Directly in front of the brilliant white light were stark silhouettes of people moving. Their voices sounded familiar yet somehow unrecognizable. They were distant and calling my name.

I began to feel lighter, as if I were floating, and my vision slowly began to return to me more clearly.

Suddenly, I could make out a mass of people standing before me - some smiling and waving, while others appeared to be crying.

When I took note of the crying people, I felt a sense of dread and fear wash over me. The smiling faces of the others gave way to sad, somber looks.

I began to feel like I was in a large freight elevator, looking out at the crowd. That's when the bottom dropped out, and I hurled downward.

At that moment, I swear that I heard my mother's voice call out. She sounded like she was in a state of misery, and I could hear her begin sobbing as I fell through the darkness.

The terror growing in me was indescribable. I was so confused, terrified really. I fell for what felt like an eternity. Just imagine the scariest drop from a rollercoaster you have ever been on; only it kept going and going and going all while picking up speed.

With a sudden and violent move, my body stopped in a jerking motion. Immediately, I felt the sensation of chains wrapping around my wrists and my ankles, suspending me above… something.

I began to feel heat come over me, but not like any heat I had ever felt before. It came at me in waves, like what you see on the road ahead on a hot July day. The chains, heavy and dense, rattled loudly whenever I tried to move.

The blackness that surrounded me seemed almost alive, moving and undulating like something from a horror movie. I could hear a distinct slithering sound but could see nothing. The heavy chains were biting more deeply into my hands and ankles with every move.

As I attempted to wriggle free, a cacophony of screams erupted below me. They began slowly and mournfully at first. Without warning, it seemed to envelope me from every angle. The screams of men, women, and what I could only guess were children.

Among the wailing, I heard a wicked noise rising up - a sound so animal and angry.

Wailing, growls, and pained sobs intensified, filling my head as I begged for it to stop. The screams would ebb and then return with a vengeance.

After hanging there for what felt like days, perhaps even weeks, my head pounded. Every muscle in my naked body screamed out for relief. Between the tortuous sounds and the flesh-ripping pain from the chains, I could not take it any longer.

The darkness was all around me, giving me the most horrific sense of isolation. Even knowing I was surrounded by voices and screams, I felt so alone and cold inside, yet my body was sweating and my flesh was burning on the outside.

Thinking it could not get worse, slithering sounds began again. I could feel something strike out at me - a sensation like long claws raking against my burning skin. They would often miss, but I could feel the rush of hot, pungent air from those unseen claws whipping past me. The horrific spasms of pain as they would find their target.

At times, the darkness would fill with a type of dark, joyous laughter, that would bellow forth from below me.

Losing my already tenuous grip on sanity, I tried in vain to cry out, but no sound emanated. At the same time, I struggled against the chains that bound me, but they refused to relent.

Without mercy, this went on for what felt like weeks. My mind was dissolving into utter madness. As I hung suspended and aching, I had what many might call a life review. Reliving moments in time - moments that brought me great shame, embarrassment, and regret.

I tried to rationalize what was happening; however, the more I did, the more fruitless it seemed. Any sense of hope I had was displaced with despair and anguish.

This must be Hell.

My devastating realization was that I had died in my yard while mowing my lawn, and this nightmare dreamscape before me was Hell.

I tried in vain to remember any prayers from my childhood, but nothing came to mind. Not even a simple prayer of grace would form in my mind.

Instead, my mind replayed every hateful thing, every nasty word I spoke, and every person I ever lashed out at. I felt their sadness, their shame, the pain - all of it - from all of them all at once. It was devastating.

To my surprise, I began to feel blows to my chest and a pain I can only describe as lightning striking me. Electricity coursed through my body. Every nerve ending was popping and jumping.

With each blast, a light appeared before my eyes.

With every brilliant, hot blast of light, I slowly began to see the faces that surrounded me. Faces locked in horrific, twisted poses, mouths agape, screaming at me, gaping, empty eye sockets staring through me filled with dark malevolence, staring at me with such hate and contempt.

The wailing of the voices was everywhere again.

FLASH. FLASH. FLASH.

The lights would streak around the room, lighting up more horrors with every flash.

I felt those damned claws continue swiping at me. The growls from below sounded more angry and animalistic than ever before. The flesh from my body was being rendered as my mind screamed in agony, and those cursed lights would flash as the pounding from inside my chest grew more intense.

Finally, battered and broken with no more hope, I hung my head and stopped resisting the bonds of the chains. The voice inside my head cried out one final time.

"I AM SORRY, SO SORRY. PLEASE GOD, JUST LET THIS END!"

Instantaneously, the pain was gone.

In fact, all sensation was gone and replaced with an eerie silence. When I say there was nothing, I mean, there…was…nothing!

Suddenly, as quickly as I had fallen, I began to feel myself rising at an inconceivable speed upwards. The cries below began again, but sounded a million miles away.

The sensation of the binding chains was gone from my wrists and ankles, but the lightning started again. Shocking, painful strikes of lightning, yet I could only see one thing - a stabbing white light that hurt my eyes and the electric crackle sound it left ringing in my ears.

Suddenly, there was a face before me. As the last flash of white light abated from my view, I could see someone, or some…thing standing before me.

That's when I heard a gentle, calming voice say, "It's not too late."

Just like that, all went black again.

I could feel my body. I could hear the background noises filter through the silence. I could hear a voice calling my name begging me to come back.

The next thing I heard was the word "CLEAR!"

My body jumped and spasmed as something against my chest filled me with electricity. My eyes opened wearily as the pain of my current situation came crashing through my senses. That glorious, manageable pain.

There I was, lying in my yard, surrounded by neighbors, police, and Emergency Medical Technicians (E.M.T.) feverishly working on me.

I looked up and saw the face of the portly, little E.M.T. working so hard to bring me back. He leaned down with a toothy smile and spoke.

"I thought I lost ya. Glad you didn't give up, Champ," he paused. "You were gone for about three to five minutes before we started working on you."

He finished as his face beamed with a righteous sense of accomplishment.

"WHAT?!" I thought. "I was dead for three to five minutes? How is that possible?" My mind cried out.

I swore that I had languished for what I knew had been weeks, maybe months, of being tormented, screamed at, and torn to pieces slowly.

Eternity means something more to me now, as I have been forced to live every minute and every second of the pain that I have caused to everyone I have ever hurt.

Now, sometimes at night, when I lay there unable to sleep, I swear I can almost hear the screams of torment. I can sometimes feel the claws trying to grab me. Thankfully, I always come back to the still, soft voice that said, "It's not too late."

God, I hope not...

"We are each our own devil, and we make this world our hell."

— *Oscar Wilde*

12

Deep Breath

My name is Andy Crump. In the summer of 2011, I had the single strangest and most unbelievable experience of my life.

I went boating with a few buddies and our girlfriends just off the shores of Malibu, CA. The day was perfect. As clouds hung lazily in the sky, it was the perfect shade of light blue. We were cradled in the rhythmic sounds of the waves lapping against our anchored boat. The laughter of friends filled the air, and the seagulls called out as they circled overhead. The sun was hot, the air was cool, and the company was lively. To say we enjoyed an adult beverage or two may be a bit of an understatement.

The day slowly gave way to night, and our floating party was just about to get its second wind. Everyone began to perk up. As we enjoyed the sunset and all that goes with it, we played games, laughed about stupid things, and enjoyed a peaceful, perfect night on the Pacific Ocean.

It was getting late - close to eleven at night - and we were going to have to head back into the dock soon to avoid a run-in with the coast guard for our boisterous gathering.

We noticed a peculiar "WHIRRING" sound. It seemed to be coming from everywhere, yet there was no discernible place at the same time. Try as we might, we could not find the source of the sound, no matter how quiet we were or in which direction we focused our attention.

About that time, my friend Dane noticed lights…under the water…flashing in a strange, nonsensical way. We watched in amazement as they began to move beneath the waves of the ocean in a strange, hypnotic dance. Our motley crew of partiers grew silent with an occasional utterance.

"What the hell are we watching?"

The glowing of the lights seemed deep and bright, but muted enough to keep us from being able to accurately pinpoint the source or get a comprehensible view of whatever was responsible for the underwater light show.

Suddenly, the night took a sharp left turn, straight into the Twilight Zone!

All the power on the boat stopped.

The lights dimmed and eventually went out, and our motor sputtered and then quit altogether.

I reached for my cell phone to shed a little light on our surroundings, but found that even our cells were non-responsive. Not a single phone among us worked.

The girls began to panic a bit while we did our best to comfort them. We were out pretty far from shore, but we could still see the lights along the beaches.

The whirring noise was back, and it was getting louder. Lights began to circle the boat at breakneck speeds. At first, the lights were white, but as they circled around us, they seemed to flicker deep blues and light purples, reds, and oranges.

The water beneath us began to churn, and the waves rocked our mid-sized craft - not enough to capsize us or even threaten to, but certainly enough to get and keep our attention.

I flicked the switch on and off for our emergency onboard radio, but my efforts proved fruitless. Everything on board was dead, and I was beginning to think we might end up the same.

The whirring noise gave way to an even stranger, electronic, humming sound as the water around us seemed to come to life, crackling with energy. I had absolutely no idea what was happening. None of us did.

At the same time, we had no clue what to do as we stood there in stunned silence. Soon, the electronic, humming sound was meshed with the quiet, gentle cries from some of my friends as we awaited an uncertain fate.

The boat began to rock a bit more violently, and the lights were getting brighter as they appeared near the surface. If this had been in the air above me, I would have been certain it was a UFO, but at this point, I had never heard of UFOs appearing underwater.

We held our breaths collectively as the glowing from beneath and around our boat stopped. The hum slowly faded, and once again, just like that, all was peaceful, except for the slightly choppy water that had been left behind.

Without warning, we felt something strike the underside of our boat. Hard. Our nerves were back on edge, sure that we were about to witness the end of our much-too-young lives. The boat began to vibrate as the thing below us continued to push against the hull.

We watched in terrified amazement as the light from below breached the side of the boat. It emerged as a large orb of brilliant white light. While it did not illuminate much around it, the light source was intense. The humming and whirring were replaced with a loud crackling noise as the ball of light hung there, motionless clicking and crackling at us.

Terrified that this thing was about to sink us, we were in full panic mode, with the girls screaming and the guys cursing. Maybe too many Sci-Fi movies influenced our fears, but they, none the less, were real.

An all-too-familiar squeezing sensation began spreading throughout my chest. Even worse, I was beginning to enter a full, anxiety-induced, asthma attack. I could feel my airways closing as my chest heaved, trying to catch a breath.

Everyone else was far too busy to notice me as they attempted to deal with their fears in their own irrational ways. In the dark, I couldn't see where to find my rescue inhaler. Terror gripped me and I dropped to my knees as I turned my attention to face this light anomaly hanging there before us.

It began to pulsate, throb, and make a high-pitched squeal. Slowly, it began to move towards me. Rightfully so, my friends began moving to the far corner of the boat. Everyone aboard was more frightened than they had ever been and convinced that they were about to be witnesses to my untimely death.

Pushing myself, I slowly began to rise with all I had to put some distance between me and IT. My knees were shaking, and my footing was uneven. I turned my back on the threat in front of me.

With my body now facing my friends, I could see the abject horror in their eyes as they watched me slowly robbed of my breath. My body was rocked, like it had been delivered a punch right in the mid-section of my back. What little air I had left in my straining lungs was expelled from my mouth with force. I dropped to my knees and then saw a brilliant flash of light exit my chest right in front of me. Soon, I was overtaken by darkness, slipping into a state of unconsciousness.

Minutes later, I woke up to my friends shaking me to rouse me from a near-death experience. The power was returned to the boat, and it was moving again as we made our way inland.

When I awoke, I gasped and drew in the deepest breath of my life. My breathing was restored. Someone must have found my inhaler and given me a few puffs while I was out of it, or so I had thought.

They told me they thought I had died, explaining that the light ball hit me and passed through my chest, leaving me in a crumpled pile on the deck. Then it dove back to the depths of the ocean, leaving no trace of its visit.

As soon as it submerged and vanished, the power to the boat flickered to life, and they scrambled to navigate our way out of this nightmare.

After our incident, I did some research and found that UFO watchers were compelled to visit this area and often claimed to see craft above the skies of Malibu and the Pacific Ocean. Some described it as the lights that would come from the water and race off through the skies. Additionally, I found that other groups meet nearby to summon these crafts, calling them forth and attempting to photograph them.

We have returned to these waters a few times since and have never had a repeat encounter with anything out of the ordinary. I will never forget what happened that day, not that I could forget if I tried. Not only did we see what we saw and experience what we experienced, but I was forever changed that day.

As a lifelong asthmatic, I have never had the need or use for my rescue inhaler again. It was like I had never had the affliction. I cannot tell you what happened that day, nor do I really care. The only thing I can say with certainty is, "Thank you."

"But remember. Just because you don't believe in something doesn't mean it isn't real."

— *Katherine Howe*

13

The Changeling

I grew up around the medieval town of Kilkenny, Ireland, which offered a rather boring and mundane life. That all changed for me when I was around 10 years old.

A lad from our town, Colin, went missing over a period of several days. This was in the mid-50s, so there was no fast way to locate someone that would vanish and no way to really make everyone aware of the dilemma in any kind of timely manner.

After word got out with the town gossips, news was all over it ,and they would craic on. It spread like a wildfire raging out of control.

I knew the boy from school. We played and spent a lot of time together, so I was truly shocked to hear the news.

People murmured that he must be dead. Some would mumble under their breath about the fairy folk secreting him away. Whatever the case, it was quite tragic and scary.

Folks from all around gathered in the city center to set about looking for the boy. It took every part of five or six days to locate him. When they did, he was found held up in a cave, lookin' as fresh as the day he went missing, like no time had passed.

A huge crowd collected around the boy, and they hit him with a barrage of questions.

"Where have ya been? Did someone take you? Are you hurt?" they asked in wild excitement.

He was unreasonably clean, not the least bit manky. The boy also looked well-nourished and hydrated. None of this seemed to make any sense. While he had not a stain on his clothes nor a scratch on his body, he had been lost, gone for nearly a week.

One thing did pop out - a very different sort of thing.

He had always had deep, dark brown eyes, but now there was a very distinct flash of green in his right eye. It was noticeable, bright, and took up a fair segment of the eye.

The other odd thing was that this boy had always been the talkative sort and was never very shy. Now, he was very quiet, very unlike himself, but who could blame him? He had, after all, been missing for a number of days. We all figured he must be in shock from the experience, but he wasn't...

It was the strangest thing, and he was very melancholy about it.

Unsettling to say the least, he said that he had no concept of how long he had been gone. His story was that he had set about exploring and wandering around when he found a shallow, inviting cave. The boy went in to have a sit. After his long day of play and exploration, he was feeling a bit knackered, so he may have nodded off for a bit. He reported that nothing extraordinary happened.

Upon further examination, the only thing the doctors found of any concern was a slight bump on the back of his head. They guessed that possibly this trauma, slight as it may be, could be responsible for his memory loss and the change in eye color, although none of us could really believe that excuse.

After a few weeks, things settled down. The town had all but forgotten or just plain moved on since, in the end, all was well.

Eventually, Colin's folks finally deemed him healthy enough to return to play, and we began hanging out again. It was easy to see that he was a different kid than he had been before, much quieter.

Additionally, there was something else off-putting about him. I just couldn't put my finger on it.

I knew something strange was going on, but it wasn't until I focused on that eye - the one brown eye that now sported that brilliant flash of green - that I realized something peculiar.

Colin never blinked.

No matter how long I tried to keep a steady gaze on him, his eyes were unblinking and cold.

He had gotten a lot faster, too.

I had always had a pretty good step on him for games like tag, but now, I'm telling you, this kid could move. Strangely, he never huffed and puffed like the rest of us, as we would eventually collapse to the ground in a sweaty, achy heap.

Instead, Colin would just stand there and stare off somewhere in the distance. It was like he was going through the motions of being a playful kid but wasn't actually enjoying the participation.

I thought maybe the bump on the head did more damage than originally believed, and that this fella was no longer the full schilling.

On one particular day, we were out with a group of us playing hide and seek. I was the seeker and had to find them all. Eventually, I did, with the sole exception being that I couldn't find Colin anywhere.

The whole lot of us took to looking for him, and slowly, we began to fear the worst - that he may have gone missing again. After a good forty minutes of hollering for him and all us kids spreading out in a desperate manner looking for him, I stumbled on a scene that I still cannot forget, no matter how hard I try.

There, behind some bushes, my friend Aeden and I located him. We stared at him in utter astonishment, taking note that Colin was there before us, stooped over a torn-apart rabbit, and to our mutual disgust, he was eating the damned thing! We stood there gawking, and our mouths hung open in complete disbelief.

He slowly turned to us. His eyes were wild, almost feral, and that dash of green took on an otherworldly glow. His face was covered in tufts of fur and blood. He almost looked a bit plastered, like he had guzzled down a few pints.

I yelled.

"Hey Boyo, you better cop on and get right with yourself!"

He just stared at us, and his voice cackled out.

"Get on with ya both!"

With that, we turned tail and got out of there in haste. I burst through the front door of my home and wasn't sure how to process what I had just seen. I needed to talk to someone about what we had just witnessed, but my parents were out, so I went to tell my Mamo about what had just occurred.

Mamo, my grandmother, was an old-timer, for sure. When I explained it all to her, she forbade me from being around Colin again. That's when she informed me that he was no longer Colin; he was a Changeling!

She explained.

"A Changeling is a creature, the offspring of a fairy, troll, elf, or other legendary beastie, that has been secretly left in the place of a human child."

She went on.

"This was the common and accepted belief of many of the ancestors when it came to the topic of a child who was taken."

I initially laughed it off, thinking Mamo was having a time pulling my leg, but she was serious - deadly serious. She continued.

"They take kids that wander off and replace them with their own kind, but are unable to replicate them perfectly."

That would explain the eyes, the weird personality shift, and the bloody mess that we had just witnessed.

Unsure of the tale Mamo just shared, I heeded her advice and left Colin alone. I never played with or hung out with him again.

Eventually, his name would pop up often in local conversation regarding some weird new tale. Some seemed fantastical, but some were outright facts. Like he was the only one that survived an electrical fire with almost no damage, but his two roommates perished in the same blaze, sleeping only ten feet away. He also survived two head-on car collisions with no injuries.

Our paths didn't cross until about 5 years ago, now well into our late 60s. He looks like he hasn't aged in 20 years.

We met at a pub for a friend's birthday gathering. I stayed away for a while, observing him, his mannerisms, and his movements. He reminded me of a lizard, cold and observing.

After tossing back a few pints, I steadied myself and decided to ask him about what happened all those years ago.

I approached him from behind, and in one swift move, he spun to face me, his hand outstretched as though he knew I was coming.

"Good to see you again, Eammon," he said as he grasped my hand in a firm shake.

I faked a smile, stared into his unblinking eyes, and nodded.

"Hello Colin….." I stammered.

He gazed deeply back into my eyes, and I swear, without moving his lips, a voice seemed to escape his mouth in a firm, authoritative growl.

"Hey Boyo, you better cop on and get right with yourself."

Colin was mocking the exact statement I had uttered to him at the last encounter with him all those years ago, there, huddled over the rabbit he was making a quick meal of.

Even through the wall of sound from the people in the pub and the Irish music blaring, I could hear his voice like it was spoken directly into my ear. Then, he smiled this distorted sort of half-grin at me, pulled me close so I could see even closer into his eyes, and they changed right there before me.

That flash of green seemed to light up as his pupils changed to slits, like an animal.

"Run along now, Boyo. Didn't your Mamo warn you about me?" he laughed.

With that, he released my hand and stepped back. I took my cue and moved quickly back to my bar stool and a waiting pint.

I sat, sweaty and nervous, then turned to scan my surroundings to see where he had gone. To my amazement, I couldn't locate him among the masses.

At this point, the birthday boy approached me along with some other friends and asked how I was and why I was keeping to myself.

"Don't ya know, this is a party, Lad," they chided.

I apologized and informed them that I just had the weirdest run-in with Colin.

My friends looked at me, bewildered.

"Colin who?" They questioned.

They informed me that he hadn't been there that night, as they would have seen and noticed him for sure. They thought I was putting them on.

Reluctantly, I returned to the party, always looking over my shoulder and scanning the room, all the while fearing another chance encounter with the changeling.

"Faery births are reportedly not only quite rare but can be extremely hazardous, so a healthy live infant is not always guaranteed, prompting faeries to steal human children instead."

– Irish Folkore

14

Nothing Is Quite As It Seems

In the fall of 1989, I enjoyed a long night of drinking and hanging out with my friends. After careful consideration, I decided that driving was <u>not</u> in my best interest.

Being responsible, I made my way around the noisy bar, saying my good-byes and goodnights and exchanging handshakes, high-fives, and hugs along the way.

Finally, I crossed the gauntlet of drunken friends, neighbors, and co-workers and reached the exit door of the bar as I heard the last person call out to me.

"See ya tomorrow, Randy!"

When I pushed open the doors to the outside, I was met with a welcoming blast of fresh, cool air. As the doors behind me closed, the sound of the party inside faded, and I set forth for my two-mile walk home. Uber and Lyft rides were not available back then, and there had been about a sixty-minute wait for a cab at this time of night.

I had walked this lonely stretch of highway many more times than I cared to admit, but it was the right thing to do. I refused to get behind the wheel of my car in this condition.

Now, when I say, "THIS CONDITION," I want it made clear. I was simply enjoying a nice mellow, but there may or may not have been some slight staggering on my walk home. My state would not be described as a fall-down, stupid drunk; instead, I was in that perfect place of in-between.

It's important for you to know that for what I am about to share with you.

As I plodded along what seemed like an endless stretch of dark road before me, I turned my hazy gaze to the skies above, thoroughly enjoying the expansive night sky.

At this point, I noticed something dark, long, and silent hovering in the sky just ahead of me. It seemed massive, maybe like a DC-10 in length, but it was a triangular shape, and it hovered there silently.

I kept my eyes fixed on the looming craft as I continued my journey.

The mix of cool, fresh air with the slow but steadily increasing boost of adrenaline was rousing me from my slightly inebriated state. My fuzzy mind was becoming sharp and inquisitive as to what it was that I was actually witnessing.

The thing that seemed so strange to me was that cars would whiz past me on the road, weary travelers seeking the safety of their homes, but no one seemed to be seeing or taking note of what I was witnessing. Maybe they were too drunk, too busy talking to passengers, or just in such a hurry to get home that they failed to cast their gaze to the heavens as I was, but I was enthralled.

As I got closer to the craft, the air seemed stale, and there was this strange muggy feeling where, moments before and simply a few yards behind me, there was a gentle cooling breeze.

Suddenly, the road around me lit up like daylight - as bright as high noon. So bright in fact that I needed to shield my eyes with my hands as I slowly tipped my head back to look for the source. The light was blinding, and my eyes squinted against the harsh, stark white light. I made a futile attempt to shield some of the light with my hand, hoping to get a better look at what was casting down the light.

When the surrounding light seemed to intensify, I squeezed my eyes tightly closed, my head still tipped back.

Moments later, I opened them again and was surprised to see that I was damn near home. The brilliant light and craft were gone.

It's important to note that the place I had stopped on the road to try to examine the source of the light had been at least a good mile - perhaps even, a mile and a quarter from my home.

Now, I was standing less than a few blocks away from my house and way too far from where I had been just moments ago.

How was this possible?

I hadn't moved, and it all happened just that fast.

I turned my attention from my neighborhood to look at my watch, and to my irritation, it had stopped at 1:18 am.

Confused, I glanced back up the road towards my house, then turned to face the direction I had just come from. I traveled a pretty good distance in the blink of an eye and had absolutely NO memory of it.

One minute, I am standing in the middle of the road, staring skyward and shielding my eyes from a brilliant light. The next second, I am a mile or so down the road.

Shaking my head in a state of puzzlement, I headed towards home, re-running the night's events through my mind, fast, then slow, then focusing even more on those moments that led to the event on the road.

Suddenly, I became acutely aware of something moving behind me and closing in.

Light footfalls crossed the pavement towards me. I turned to see who was heading my way at this rapid pace.

To my astonishment, it was a short figure with a huge head, giant black orb-like eyes, not almond-shaped, and there were rounded black pools of weirdness. It kept moving toward me with determination when I somehow found the courage to yell.

"HEY, MAN. BACK OFF!"

To my amazement, it stopped in its tracks.

Like a confused puppy, its head tilted to the side as if it were sad for having been spoken to so harshly.

A few hundred yards back down the road from where I had been, light struck the pavement. It began traveling silently but swiftly through the air. There was a sound of rushing wind, but nothing mechanical. No engine, just wind moving like a storm was blowing in at breakneck speed.

My new little friend looked toward the light, then turned to face me again. Its face looked much less friendly this time. As the light fell closely behind it, the being lowered its head down and began to charge me.

Unsure of what to do, I steadied and prepared myself to kick this freaky little fella into next week if he kept running up on me.

It seemed the closer he got, the slower he moved, and the louder the roar of the wind became.

I positioned myself to give this alien one hell of a kick.

As it approached, it looked up at me with its mouth turned downward in a cross between pain and rage. Without a second thought, I let my leg go, unleashing the fury to full-on kick him when, at that exact moment, the light hit me.....

I was surrounded by the sound of crashing glass as my foot connected with the vase on my coffee table in my living room, sending it flying across the room and directly into the opposing wall, hard causing the vase to shatter into hundreds of pieces.

The light in my living room flickered on, and my roommate came running into the living room, baseball bat in hand, demanding to know what the hell just happened.

I turned and looked at him.

"I...uhh, I don't know. I seriously don't know." I replied in a quizzical manner.

"A minute ago, I was on the road, down the block, about to give a swift kick to something charging at me. Next thing I know, my kick connected to the vase, and here I am in my living room," I finished.

He looked at me like I had lost my damn mind.

I heard him mutter as he turned away to go back to his room.

"Drunken idiot!"

I stood there at a complete loss for logic, wondering, "what the hell just happened to me?"

Eventually, I made my way to the bathroom and decided to take a quick, hot shower.

As I pulled my shirt over my head, I was baffled to see a series of red dots forming a triangle on my chest. Blood trickled from one of the wounds.

I lifted my finger to the bleeding hole and touched it.

With that swift movement, I was met with white, hot blinding pain, which caused me to let out a scream of pain. When I did, I suddenly and inexplicably found myself sitting bolt upright in my bed.

A violent thumping began on my wall.

Three loud bangs.

BANG. BANG. BANG.

For the briefest of moments, I was terrified and unable to move. That's when I heard my roommates muffled yell from the next room.

"Keep it down in there. Jesus, people are trying to sleep."

I shook my head in a futile attempt to clear the cobwebs of confusion.

Laying there, I reached to my chest and found scabbed-over wounds that now appeared days old.

I thought, "Am I losing my mind?"

Half-convinced that I truly was going insane, I laid back and closed my eyes. My mind whirled, trying to make sense of all the strange activities that had happened.

As I found myself beginning to fall asleep out of pure exhaustion, I saw it.

That face.

Those big, round black eyes.

The turned-down, opened mouth that emanated a loud, ear-shattering noise that sounded like...... an alarm clock.

My alarm clock.

When I opened my eyes, I was alone in the room, an alarm blaring next to me. I hit the off button and stared at the clock in amazement.

It was 11am..... two days later!

"...and it is our fear of our regrets that causes our fear of the visitors."
— *Whitley Strieber*

And here we are, dear readers. You have made it through this book of supernatural shenanigans, but before I bid you farewell, what say you? Shall I regale you with one more tale from my own personal experiences before we part? I call this one…

15

In My Room

My room was filled with visitors and medical staff alike, all stopping by to check on my recovery after an emergency gallbladder removal. The pain was unreal, and I was connected to a wonderful pain reduction system (Morphine drip) and with the push of a button, could control my own pain/pleasure principle…and control it…or perhaps over-control it, I did.

It was at this point in my stay that I started to notice a very strange situation unfolding in my hospital room. I realized that aside from the constant flow of visitors and nurses checking on me, I had, unbeknownst to the others in my room, a large gathering of shadowy figures watching over me. They were patiently waiting for those moments when I would "see" them, and they would attempt to communicate.

Now, I know what you are all thinking: drugs, hallucinations, and wild imagination. I cannot for certain disagree; however, I know that those moments when I could see them are as burned in my memory more clearly than the conversations and interactions I was having with my living, breathing, flesh and blood visitors.

Never before had I ever experienced such a strange and surreal situation. You see, while my eyes were open, I could see, hear, and communicate with all my fleshy, warm-blooded visitors and medical staff, but when my eyes closed... I could still see every detail of my room, except for the actual people in it.

I could still hear the people that were there in my room and interact with them, but they were no longer in my visual spectrum. I was acutely aware of the pinging of machines, the monitor alarms sounding throughout the hospital and the overhead page system calling doctors to their stations. But within my hospital room, there was another faction of guests that I could only see. (Yes, I am aware of how ludicrous this is about to sound.)

Now, as I was saying before, I was so rudely interrupted by me that I could only see these other beings with my eyes closed. It was as though my third eye was fully open, and taking in all the unseen around me. I had fully engaged my sixth sense.

My hospital room was filled with ashen-faced, silent beings, many of whom stood there watching me; only a few would move. Among them, there was the being that I call "The Woman," a wild-haired, elderly woman who would float there in front of my face. Her hair seemed to be blowing by some unseen force, her eyes were piercing, and her face was filled with lines and anguish.

She would stare deeply into my eyes, mouthing words in a silent scream that I could not hear, insisting that I pay attention to her. She grew angrier and more persistent as my stay continued, which also led me to believe that this was more, so much more than a drug-filled hallucination.

My conscious, or perhaps subconscious, was wide open to another level of existence, and these spirits knew it. They could sense that I was straddling two realms, and being opportunists, they were making sure that I would see and remember everything.

On one specific day, a friend came to visit me. He brought me some snacks and some things to read. I remember thinking how nice it was to see him. We shared some small talk and chit-chatting, mostly about my need for attention and faking this illness in order to take time off from work.

"You better take care of yourself and get your ass back to work and on the air!" he insisted with a smile.

The dreamy effects of the morphine drip were causing my eyelids to begin to grow heavier and slam shut from time to time. Tim would let out a laugh and poke fun at me.

"Morphine, it's a hell of a drug, huh, D?" he would say, and we would laugh as I fought to keep my eyes open.

We spoke about my son's impending wedding that weekend and how he was willing to give me a piggy-back ride to the nuptials if I needed one. I replied with a smirk and a snicker, then slowly, my eyes closed. I could see the alternate view of my room, devoid of Tim, my girlfriend, or my son.

My head slowly pivoted in the opposite direction of my "living" friends and family, and I began to focus on the corner of the room where my less lively roommates had congregated.

One moved forward and pointed at me, his long finger wagging and his mouth obviously moving in an unheard conversation. All I think I could hear was this creepy hissing noise emanating from his mouth while the others appeared to speak in hushed whispers. I could not make out, but that seemed to fill the room. I spoke out.

"I'm sorry, I just can't hear you. I wish I could. I see your mouths move, but I cannot hear a word you are trying to say."

I heard Tim's concerned voice question me.

"Hey D, I am over here. Ummm, who are you talking to?"

I then informed him that there were a lot of people here in my room wanting to be heard.

There was a bit of a pregnant pause, and I heard his voice cut through the surreal haze of my experience. Only this time, all the spirits in my room turned to face him as well.

"Hey buddy...there is no one over there," he assured me. "We are all over here on this side of the room."

I laughed and said, "Good thing you are, cuz it's pretty crowded over here.

And that was when I informed everyone in my room that I could only see them when I closed my eyes.

There was another hesitation, then Tim retorted.

"Dave, are you kidding around? Everything okay, brother?"

My head turned wearily to the sound of his voice. It was so odd. I could hear him so clearly, but visually, I could not see him. Yet, in the other part of my room, I could see the throngs of creepy roommates that I had amassed but could not hear them.

My eyes popped open briefly as I looked directly into the face of my worrisome friend.

"It's all good, Tim. Morphine IS a hell of a drug!" And with that, our conversation came to an abrupt end.

My eyes once again dreamily closed, and I heard him tell my girlfriend.

"I am going to head out. Let me know how he is doing. That was really weird."

For days after I was released, I wracked my brain trying to understand what I had witnessed in the hospital and often found myself vacillating between belief and disbelief of what it was I experienced.

I tried so hard to convince myself that everything I saw and experienced was the machinations of a drug-induced haze, but I could remember it all so clearly and so vividly. That has always stuck with me.

This experience sent me down a rabbit hole that I have yet, all these years later, been unable, or perhaps fully willing, to pull myself out of. I tried to understand or comprehend what is going on around us - the unseen forces that always permeate the world.

Are we just that close to another reality or dimension? Do the dead really surround us? Then, my heart sank as I thought about a room full of the ashen, washed-out ghosts, trapped, caught between this world and the next, filling the rooms and halls of hospitals, asylums, and institutions around the world. How many millions, or hundreds of millions, of spirits must still walk their halls?

What I found most disturbing was why they were still here, walking among us, especially in places like that. I would hope that in the end, if I stay on as a ghost, I will be bouncing between visiting my kids and scaring some investigators at an old asylum or prison.

Why do spirits choose to stay or allow themselves to get stuck in these circumstances? My only solace came from a fellow investigator and researcher who shed some light on what may come next and why those that stay are still here.

It was a packed bar, filled with muted conversations lost over the sound of 80s music playing through the speakers, when my dear friend, Misty Bay, looked deeply into my eyes and spoke.

"When we die, all that we are, all the good, the promise, the light will go on and complete its journey. Wherever that journey may be, and that which is left behind, is the anger, the resentment, jealousy, pettiness, the base, the animal instinct part of all of us."

She paused.

"That may be why communication is often short and limited to bangs, flickering lights, and an occasional *"GET OUT"* and why most communication is so basic. It leaves behind the animal part of us, the pack mentality of sticking with others like itself in an environment that it is familiar with, until at some point that energy fades and finally goes out like a match in a breeze."

I looked at her. After a few moments of just sitting with that explanation, I posed the following question:

"Then, what happens to the light of us, the best of us?"

Without missing a beat, she lifted the beer bottle to her lips, took another long pull from it, and said, "Now, that is the REAL question, isn't it?"

With that, we sat in silence, enjoying our libations and reflecting on the concepts of what may lie beyond.

AFTERWORD

So, as I leave you now, my little Darklings, try to comfort yourselves with the thought that as you hear tales of lost spirits, the communication and the reality that seems to be pushing itself into our realm, take a moment to realize that, much like Jacob Marley warned as he rattled his chains in dire warning to Ebenezer Scrooge in Charles Dickens' A Christmas Carol.

"The chains we forge in this life, we must carry on to the next."

Be kind to yourself and to others. Work on shortening those chains, and make this life right while you have the chance instead of leaving a dark and tortured version of yourself behind bonded to this Earth by all the negativity we create for ourselves daily.

Maybe the longer you allow the negative in and to surround you, the longer that part of you will stay behind until it fades.

Welcome to a world of possibilities, of nightmares and hope, and welcome to the reality that is….. The Paranormal.

Until next we meet…..

*Farewell and may you live in an abundance of laughter and of love with a few healthy scares along the way to keep you on your toes. – **Dave Schrader***

ABOUT THE AUTHOR

From an early age, Dave Schrader has been surrounded by the strange and anomalous, from haunted homes to creature sightings, UFO encounters, and more. Now, as an experienced paranormal investigator, he travels the world seeking the truth and following the claims of Ghosts, Bigfoot, UFOs, Monsters, Myths and Legends.

You can also see Dave streaming on MAX & Discovery+'s hit TV series, *The Holzer Files* and *Ghosts of Devil's Perch.* Dave has also appeared on *Paranormal State, Ghost Adventures, Ghost Adventures: Screaming Room, Paranormal Challenge, Haunted Hospitals*, *Fright Club* and in the ShockDocs; *The Curse of Lizzie Borden* & *Demon in the White House.*

Dave has lived in Minnesota for thirty-five years with his family, which includes eleven children and eight grandchildren. He has been a mainstay of local radio on KLBB, KTLK, WCCO, *Coast to Coast AM* and as host of his own podcast, *The Paranormal 60*.

Dave invites you along on his journey and thanks you for taking him along on yours. You can find out more about Dave at www.Paranormal60.com.

Made in the USA
Columbia, SC
19 February 2024

32018489R00080